Having a Job Just Like Recess

Having a Job Just Like Recess

A Parent's Manual for Guiding and Gracing Your Child's Career Path

By
Mark H. de Roo

Writers Club Press
New York Lincoln Shanghai

Having a Job Just Like Recess
A Parent's Manual for Guiding and Gracing Your Child's Career Path

Writers Club Press
an imprint of iUniverse, Inc.

For information address:
iUniverse
2021 Pine Lake Road, Suite 100
Lincoln, NE 68512
www.iuniverse.com

ISBN: 0-595-26168-X (Pbk)
ISBN: 0-595-65543-2 (Cloth)

Printed in the United States of America

Dedication

This book is dedicated to those four people
who make coming home each night
the highlight of my day:
my wife and children,
Roxanne, Ingrid, Taylor, and Hillary.

Table of Contents

Preface

Let's start with a question. What are the two most feared words to a college pre-med student? '*Organic Chemistry.*'

Whether a pre-med college freshman is successful or not in this course is akin to "Go. Collect $200" or "Go directly to jail." It's either sink or swim. There simply is no middle ground. You either got no less than a B+ in Organic Chem or you could kiss a medical career good bye. No pressure, right?

When I was a freshman at Hope College, a number of my classmates (I not among them, thank goodness) claimed "Pre-Med" as their likely college major. But it was more than a major. For some, it was their ticket to a truly worthy profession. For others, it was competency to be combined with their call to a future mission field. For most, however, it was their ticket to "the good life." Pursuing a possible medical career was not a hasty decision either. It was something talked about, encouraged to, or almost mandated by Mom or Dad.

A pre-med student at Hope College would know soon enough in their college career. You took the course either first semester or if you could delay the agony long enough, second semester would be the latest. It was what I witnessed at the conclusion of each semester that lingers almost 30 years later. For some, the euphoria of getting an "A" in the class was the closest thing to winning the $100 million Power Ball lottery. Those with less than a B+ were destined or doomed to other things. Their devastation was huge: tears, lonely walks, and in some cases, immediate trips to the Registrar's Office to drop out of school.

So, question #2. Did this have to be? Why did so much have to hinge on one solitary course? Yeah, I know rules are rules and weeding-out mechanisms are part of life. Yet, I need to approach this question from another angle. Why were so many of my classmates taking a course and pursuing a major unnecessarily so? It seemed to me at that time and even more so three decades hence that many of these students could have saved themselves the pressure if they had simply been more honest with themselves. Maybe, *honest* is too harsh a word. Let's try *authentic.*

You and I both know that not everyone is meant to grow up to be President. Or, CEO of Microsoft. Or, a carpenter. Or, an architect. Yet, for many of my classmates at Hope College wearing the mask of future M.D. was the only option. If these students had simply taken some time to evaluate more of *who* they are and less of *what* to be, well the first year burden of a pre-med student would have been prevented and better channeled somewhere else.

But who among us at age 17 is so wise to recognize this and its life-long implications? Let's be honest. Not many. As teenagers go, many have a hard time figuring out what do on a Friday night, let alone their life's calling. But, let's not be too harsh. The late teens are fraught with gobs of issues, questions, and demands. Today, young people, even prior to the teen years, are faced with pressures on what to wear, how to look, what to see, what to listen to, and what to play.

And then, there's the issue of what to *be.* So, many young people aspire to what they see on *ER* or what they read in *People.* More often than not, however, there are the throngs of young people who have little, if any, clue on what their career calling might be. The "I don't know what I want to do" mantra for most young people then becomes something left to chance. Yes, our schools make some limited effort at career development, but due to numbers and finances, the emphasis is on "limited." When we take this type of scenario to its logical conclusion, it shouldn't surprise any one of us that 83% of working adults fail to finds both personal and financial satisfaction in their career (Roper Study).

So, one more question and, believe me, this is the last one: If a young person is clueless about what to do and our schools have limited resources to provide career assistance, who is best suited to provide career direction and assistance? The answer should be apparent: parents. And this should come as no surprise. As parents, we certainly desire happiness for our children in other aspects of their lives, including their families, their marriages, and in their communities. Why wouldn't we desire an equal measure of satisfaction for our children in their work?

Some of a parent's uncertainty about how to facilitate a measure of career assistance stems from viewing this as a parent's role. After all, a parent wears so many other hats: doctor, disciplinarian, nutritionist, psychologist, coach, entertainer, educator, etc.

But, how about "career counselor?"

For most parents, that one doesn't fit as comfortably. Many parents admonish kids to take the easy route and merely have them do what they're doing. On the other hand, there are parents who direct their children to careers they one time wished for themselves. And of course, there are parents who believe the only career worth anything is one whose annual bottom line is nothing less than six figures. Other parents are a bit more noble but whose career guidance for their children is confined to these simple words, "You'll be good at anything you want to do." While such support is well-intended, it lacks the substance that results in enabling your child to step onto a meaningful and successful career path, regardless of whether that path has M.D., C.P.A. or C.N.A. (certified nurse assistant) beside it. Perhaps, if a bit more time, attention, and tools were given to the parents of those clients, those individuals would not have experienced the degree of burnout, confusion, and lack of direction in their careers that caused them to call me.

Having a Job Just Like Recess provides those tools. It offers ideas and insights for parents of a child at any age. You will experience ways to discern the fabric of your children that will make for more appropriate—more authentic—career choices. And, of course, we begin with a basic premise. We have to recognize that each of us—parent and child—is part of God's creation whose greater Purpose can be fulfilled through our vocations. If we are able to do this for each other and especially for our kids, then we will be much closer to realizing what St. Paul meant when saying, *You are God's workmanship, created in Jesus Christ, to do good works which He prepared, in advance, for you to do.* (Ephesians 2: 10).

Acknowledgements

This book is born out of experience.

Early in my career as a career counselor, I began to ask my clients a question: "To what degree did your parents influence your career either through discussions, experiences, or something more?" In no less than 99% of the time, the answer was either "Not at all" or "Very little." While this might be disappointing, it's not surprising. After all, I don't know many people who were given *The Ultimate Parents' Manual* with a chapter on "Career Planning." Nevertheless, these clients had the courage initially to pick up the phone and call me to schedule an appointment. Their insights, frustrations, and reflections helped spawn the idea for this book. To these clients—all 800 of them—I express my appreciation.

I also want to thank a couple of good friends. Bob Tennant for his friendship and his weekly encouragement. To Paul Prins, for his optimism and willingness to edit parts of the book in its early stages. A significant expression of thanks goes to Dr. David Myers from Hope College. His successful venture into writing, coupled by some practical how-to's for yours truly, served as necessary and helpful mile markers along the way.

My parents also deserve a word of thanks. Their occasional inquiry, "So, how's the book coming?" provided a measure of implicit accountability. Parents do those things, you know.

Lastly, I want to thank my Roxanne, my wife, plus Ingrid, Taylor, and Hillary, my children for their patience. My weekly Saturday and Sunday afternoons to the library over more years than I want to admit showed significant tolerance and flexibility on their part. While not actively involved in the editing process, they fueled me with ideas, perspective, and helpful doses of cheerleading, which are critical for anyone running a writing marathon. Thanks, guys.

Introduction

In early March of 1993, I received a letter at work from a social service agency, informing me of the national "Take Your Daughter to Work Day" that would be occurring later in the month. Actually, the letter wanted me to promote this day within my company's workforce. As Director of Human Resources at the time, hardly a day went by without some type of similar correspondence that was promoting something, wanting something (otherwise known as "money"), or requesting volunteers. Many were touting activities—OK, fund raising events—from a United Way Annual Dinner to Donkey Basketball games. I couldn't fault their causes, but I have to confess that I pitched most of these letters.

I didn't toss that March, '93 letter, however. I figured that this day would allow a little healthy father/daughter "bonding" between myself and my thirteen-year-old daughter, Ingrid. It would allow her to taste, see, and hear a manufacturing environment. Well, she jumped at the chance but for her own reasons. First, it got her out of school for half a day. Secondly, she got a free lunch. Typical motives for most thirteen-year-olds, I suppose.

So, we did it. I guess the day proved mildly successful at best. The morning part—the shadowing experience—for Ingrid was kind of a "downer." She said the stamping presses made too much noise and those wide-body safety glasses weren't too cool. Lunch wasn't much better either. All attendees at the event corralled at noon in the fellowship hall of a local church for, well, guess what? A box lunch. You know the standard fare. Chicken salad on a croissant, carrot strips, an apple, a brownie, and a drink box. I tried to console her by suggesting that maybe next year they'd have pizza. Her response: "Nice try, Dad."

Lunch was concluded by some obligatory remarks from the event's coordinator as well as a short speech by Dr. Charles "Chuck" Muncatchy, a local superintendent. As superintendents go, Chuck is one of the best. He is creative, results-oriented, technology-minded, and great with kids. He's also one to "walk his talk," including this particular day when he, too, brought his own teenage daughter to his job and the luncheon. Well, after unintentionally embarrassing her (Dads have a special way of doing this) at the beginning of his remarks, he started with a story.

He conveyed an incident where, in the process of touring one of his district's elementary schools a few weeks earlier, he came upon a ten-year old girl in the school's computer lab. Apparently, his entering the lab failed to create a distraction for this fourth grader. Her attention to the computer screen was not to be denied. Yet, there was something even more striking about this scene. The young girl's smile. The ear-to-ear type. It was so genuine that Chuck had to interrupt her by saying, "Say, I'm sorry to bother you, but I couldn't help but noticing that you seem to be really enjoying this computer." She promptly replied, "Oh yes. This is fun! In fact, it's so much fun, it's just like recess!"

Computers and recess? Computers and smiles? Aren't those concepts mutually exclusive? OK, I'll admit to being no computer aficionado. Computers and I are a long way away from any sort of a relationship. Yet, not so for this ten-year old girl.

I wish I could give you a few more details from the rest of the superintendent's remarks. I can't. Somehow, the story about that little girl immediately began to stir in my mind while he was talking. It played with my mind. It poked a lot of assumptions. It also sparked some ideas. Among those was a simple concept of encountering someone having pure pleasure when performing an activity.

From this, I found myself asking some questions. I mean, lots of questions. What causes some people to truly enjoy certain tasks over others? Why do some people like to dabble with computers and others with people's minds (e.g. psychologists or therapists)? Why does Glenn, my auto mechanic, seem to have a love affair with our family van's Mitsubishi engine? Why does my artist-friend get lost in fashioning some colorful pieces of stained glass? Why am I impressed with my minister's agility and his playfulness in delivering so many insightful words-of-wisdom Sunday after Sunday?

Two more questions. Could it be that these people are experiencing pure pleasure by integrating *who* they are in *what* they do? And could this pleasure be as much fun as a ten-year old during recess?

Noted author, James Michener, thinks so. He once commented, "The master in the art of living makes little distinction between his work and his play, his labor and his leisure, his mind and his body, his information and his recreation, his love and his religion. He hardly knows which is which. He simply pursues his vision of excellence at whatever he does, leaving others to decide whether he is working or playing. To him, he's always doing both."

If only that could be the case for most of us. A study by the Roper Institute in 1992 revealed that only 12% of working Americans find both personal and financial satisfaction in their current occupation. What a tragedy! That's 88 out of 100 persons who come home after work either bored, bummed, or burned out. If you're an employer, that is 88% of your workforce whose lack of excitement or commitment might be reflected in poor product quality, late deliveries, or substandard service—not an enticing thought in the eyes of your customers. Or, if you're our nation's Secretary of Labor, you're all-too-aware of an increasing number of countries outperforming, outproducing, and underpricing our own industrial base. And, what does that suggest for our country's standard of living?

If you're part of that 88%, watch out! You'll likely become a victim—if you haven't already. Corporate America is restructuring, reengineering, and reinventing itself in ways a previous generation would have thought impossible and unethical. Gone are the cradle-to-grave loyalties between company and employee. The demise of this social contract has left a wake of people who are stung, bewildered, and cynical. At best, many persons are skeptical of the companies or institutions they believed would tend their careers. These same people might even be a bit resentful of their parents who advised, "Treat them (the company) right, and you'll do right by them."

But, don't blame Mom and Dad. The rules have changed. The playing field has changed. Career management has changed. It's left only one alternative: self-management. We now realize that all of us must be navigators of our careers, particularly if we are going to keep abreast of the 8-10 jobs and the 2-3 career shifts we'll likely experience in our lives.

Chances are you've heard all this already. However, is it a message you find frightening or enticing? Perhaps, you've answered that by reading one of a host of excellent books on "Managing a Mid-Career Shift," "Winning Resumes," "How to Start Your Own Business," etc. While well intentioned, my suspicion about most of these books is that they tend to veil lots of larger issues—issues that deal with the "biggies" in life, the kind of proverbial building blocks on which any career must be meaningfully constructed. These are biggies like a purpose in life, personal identity, and our gifts.

OK, you're saying, "I understand the parts about a purpose in life and personal identity. But, 'gifts?'"

Yes, gifts—as in talents, aptitudes, and abilities. Listen to author Elizabeth O'Connor who in her book, *Gifts and Creativity*, suggests "When we talk about the person we are intended to be, we are talking about gifts. We cannot be ourselves without being true to our gifts. Whenever we struggle with what we are to do in life, we are struggling to uncover our talent or gift."

Too often, that struggle is too much like work. So, we defer it. Too frequently we yield our personal identity to a best buddy, peer pressure, or what's "hot." It's particularly unfortunate when the direction for our lives can be so easily found within ourselves where Someone has placed it.

In a very special way, each of our gifts has been inscribed into us. It's a unique impression with a distinctive thumbprint attached. That thumbprint is no less than the fingerprint of God.

It is the good Lord who has bestowed a combination of talents, preferences, and gifts that distinguishes each of us from each other. Gifts—not race, gender, or traditions—make for differences between worker and co-worker, between my minister and my mechanic, and between myself and my children. Any type of career or life planning must begin with this recognition.

Beyond this fact, however, is the "how" question. What's the procedure and how do we merge who we are with what we should do in our career? Let's be honest, wouldn't it be simple and convenient if there was a basic "how-to" career planning manual that would be promptly handed to us at birth. I'd even settle for one as a high school graduation gift. OK, if there wasn't a handbook, maybe there could be designated persons who could guide, enable, and encourage us in the process.

Thank goodness, there are! They're called "parents." And as a reader of this book, you're probably one of them.

If you're a typical parent, I think it's safe to assume that you only want the best for your children and their lives. The "best" usually translates into meaning good schools, good friends, a loving future spouse (if marriage is in the picture), and certainly a good job. As parents, we usually help them with their homework and maybe even who they hang out with. But, let's be honest, a good parent does not necessarily a good career counselor make.

That's the purpose of this book. While you won't earn a Ph.D. in Career Education, you'll add to your repertoire of parenting skills by becoming a "career enabler." The chapters, stories, questions, and yes, assignments (but don't sweat it!) are intended to assist you with three pretty important activities:

1) Identifying and affirming your child's gifts, aptitudes, and preferences,

2) Channeling their gifts into some appropriate career options, and
3) Doing so with a recognition that a career can be fun (like recess!) and purposeful.

The book is divided into three sections without defined borders. The first two chapters provide an appropriate framework for assisting both you and your child's career planning activities. Chapter I will likely challenge most traditional thinking about career management and will offer ways to make this book a little less like work. Chapter II suggests some basic parenting tips to make both your message and the messenger (you) consistent and genuine.

The next several chapters are intended to give you some important method to uncover, identify, and link your children's aptitudes and preferences with some meaningful career options. Chapter III highlights the importance of involvement, experiences, and opportunities as mediums to making visible your child's talents and gifts. Ways to more definitively dissect and put names to your child's talents and preferences are offered in Chapter IV. Chapter V points to some connections between your child's profile and specific careers; you'll need some pencils and paper for this chapter.

The final four chapters offer other dimensions that will complete the circle. Chapter VI aims to dispel a number of myths about some important persons in our lives: young women, persons of color, people with disabilities, and the gifted and talented. This chapter will also provide some special career planning tips that are specific to each person. The following chapter suggests ways for you to work with your child's school to make career management and self-awareness more significant. The future is the focus in Chapter VIII as we explore changes to specific careers, the workplace, and the way we work. And lastly, considering work as more than just a paycheck—as something with a Divine purpose—is the topic for Chapter IX.

Blended into the book are stories. The true-to-life type. You'll hear from United States Congressman, an author of children's books, and a

Midwest hospital CEO, among others. Each person will share how their mother or father or both parents have significantly or subtly influenced his or her career. I hope you'll find their accounts to be as fascinating and instructional as I have.

One final introductory comment. If you doubt that parents influence a child's career choice, listen to the following story.

The dateline is 1880. A pastor of the United Brethren Church makes several visits to his parishioners in and around his family's home in Richmond, Indiana. Whether it was at a yard sale, a general store, or from a local craftsman, the bishop purchases a small toy between visits. The simple toy is a semi-mechanical type with a small weight attached to a string. When dropped, the resulting action turns some blades reminiscent to the wings of a windmill, similar to that of a propeller.

It's late on this particular day and the bishop is anxious to get home. Upon his arrival, he promptly gives the new toy to his two boys. One son is 11 years old, the other 7. To see these two boys receive this gift, well, you might have thought it was ten Christmases wrapped up in one! For hours, the boys play and ponder this new treasure. Little did these guys suspect, however, that those few hours would actually stretch into a lifetime.

You see, these two boys' fun also sparked a lot of imagination and possibilities. They began to ask lots of "what if" questions. And eventually, their inquiries and speculations lead to a place called Kitty Hawk—and a new fangled contraption labeled an "aeroplane." You undoubtedly know the rest of the story.

It all began with a simple act. An act of giving from a father to his sons. My suspicion, however, is that Mr. Wright, the good pastor, didn't merely leave the kids to have all the fun. He probably played with them with the same level of excitement and fascination as the two boys. And in the process of sharing that toy, the guys peppered him with questions like, "Dad, how do these things go round and round? Why do I feel air blowing behind and not in front of it? Dad, what about……" Undoubtedly, the blend of giving and active involvement by the father may have been the critical factor in the imaginations of Orville and Wilbur Wright.

A simple act. An extraordinary result. What it points out is that whether it's simple or grandiose, subtle or intentional, parents can—and do—influence kids and their careers. That opportunity is an act of giving that only a Mom or Dad can know. It's called love. And the opportunity is now because the future is theirs—a future with a Purpose.

Chapter I

The 3 R's to Successful Career Planning for Kids

Everyone has "Top 10" lists, right? Those lists seem to range from personal "Top 10 Books," "Top 10 Vacation Spots," to "Top 10 Out-of-the-Way Places to Eat." And, of course, everyone has a Top 10 list on their favorite movies. So do I. It's really hard for me to nail down my number one movie but somewhere near the top is one from the late 80's called *Dead Poets' Society*.

For me, it's a classic. Based on an actual experience of a literature teacher at a New England prep school, Professor John Keating, a.k.a. Robin Williams, inspires and challenges his students in the most non-traditional of ways. Keating's first few days with his new brood of students are memorable. On one of those days, he begins his discussion on poetry by asking one of the students to read aloud the Introduction to their textbook. In an introduction that sounds more like a 10-step set of instructions on how to assemble my lawnmower, the author believes that great poetry can be assessed by means of a mathematical formula. The author, a J. Evans Pritchert, Ph.D., contends that a reader can assess such greatness by rating both the poetry's "importance" and its "perfection" and multiplying the two to obtain a score. Let's pick up the good professor's critique just after the student has finished reading the introduction:

Professor Keating: *"Garbage. That's what I think of Mr. J. Evans Pritchert. We're not laying pipe here. Now I want you to rip out that page. Go on! Rip out the entire page! Shred. Tear. We'll put it on a roll! Go ahead, rip it out!*

What follows is pandemonium in the classroom. I mean, who wouldn't relish the opportunity to give a literal rip at a few pages of a book (this one excluded, thank you!). Even though the students have a blast in the process, Professor Keating's purpose is not to disparage poetry. Not by a long shot. Rather, he suggests there are different ways to approach a subject whether it's poetry, physics, or introductory mechanics. For the good professor, a "new and improved" perspective was needed if the material was to count for anything. By doing so, he hoped his bunch of preppies might even get turned on to something as seemingly non-utilitarian as poetry. And, of course, they did.

In a similar way, a fresh approach is fundamental when connecting the whole career planning process to you and your children. Yeah, rip out those old prescriptions, road maps, or "this is what you will do when you grow up" mentality. Career planning is not intended to be a one-time event or a B-O-R-I-N-G chore that sounds too much like work itself.

I think what follows will help. I call them "The 3 R's to Successful Career Planning for Kids." You can interpret them as reference points or reminders. They're also meant as ingredients. Perhaps, you'll view them as some sort of a spice. Personally, I think of them as yeast. If used, they'll help the process immeasurably. And, the results will be much more bountiful.

Let's cook!

The First "R": Reframing

To describe our first reference point—our first "R"—you'll need a pencil. The instructions are simple. You are to connect the nine dots below with four connecting lines. The key word is connecting. Once you place your pencil on the paper, you can't remove it. Give yourself about 30 seconds to do it. OK, enough begging, I'll give you a minute. Please do it now.

o o o

o o o

o o o

........Time's up! Right now, you're either feeling accomplished, frustrated, or groveling for more time to complete it. Even if you didn't get it, you're probably suspecting that you have to go outside the dots to connect them all. Well, you're right. (For the correct answer, see item A in the Appendix).

I've heard various labels attached to this exercise, but the one I prefer is "reframing." If I had mentioned this earlier in the title to this section, it might have given you a clue about how to complete the Nine Dot exercise. Nevertheless, it's fairly simple to see why it has this name. When first viewing these 9 dots, we subconsciously connect the outer dots with a perimeter of imaginary lines to create a frame or a box. To achieve the task, however, you had to break out of that natural frame of reference. You had to "reframe."

"Reframing" conveys three important messages. First, as much as it is common to have some standard and familiar ways of approaching certain tasks, not everything should submit to "Standard Operating Procedures." That's particularly true when it comes to planning our careers. For most of us, career planning has been confined to either a six week mini-course in the ninth grade, reading the Sunday classified ads, or subscribing to someone's casual comment, "You know, you'd be good as a __________." For some people, this works well. For most, it doesn't. And, the results are a collection of disenchanted workers.

It certainly doesn't have to be this way. It most certainly shouldn't be this way for your children. Rather, career planning for your children should be a process of engagement, exposure, experience, and affirmation. But more on that later in the book.

The second and third messages are found in those two outer, imaginary dots that had to be created in order to complete the exercise. Both are symbolic but poignantly so. Again, in order to achieve the puzzle, you had to leave that self-imposed, imaginary box. You had to depart from the familiar. You were forced to alter your perceptions in order to make something happen. Sometimes, we have to do that with people. Let me explain.

In the course of interviewing candidates for positions or clients in counseling sessions, I frequently ask them to offer some adjectives that describe themselves. The descriptions usually include such words as "hard-working," "good with people," and "nice." Pretty standard responses. Unfortunately, such responses often reflect a fairly limited self-perception. You see, most people can generally develop a list of three or four words to characterize themselves, but when you probe them for more, it's a major struggle. How unfortunate when the sum and substance of our self-perceptions are mostly narrow, ordinary, and lukewarm. More importantly, it's almost tragic because individuals, including our children, are so much more than a few standard adjectives.

Seeing things beyond the standard and commonplace recently came to me in, of all places, a deli called *The Corner Bakery* in Union Station in Chicago. While waiting for the train, we decided to get a couple of sandwiches prepared for our return trip to Michigan. Conspicuous by its absence was anything akin to standard white bread. Apparently, the bakers in the particular deli viewed bread as anything but ordinary. In fact, here is their stated philosophy:

> "You only knead a few things in life.....ciabatta, baguette, figs, honey, wheat berry, olive fougasse, walnuts, Italian thyme, dill, raisins, pecans, rye, cherry country sourdough....."

There's more, but you get the idea. Anyway, these are people who are juiced by bread! For them, bread is romanced by these many and anything-but-ordinary ingredients. And because of it, I tasted and savored the best sandwich of my life. By the way, is it time for lunch yet?

People, too, can be either white or multi-grain. I once asked two middle school teachers what they felt particularly skilled at doing as teachers. One teacher commented, "I guess I'm pretty good at working with kids, at least the good ones." Contrast that sentiment with the next teacher who said, "I really enjoy being with twelve to fourteen year olds, probably because I get to wear so many hats: entertainer, counselor, friend, and, of course, teacher. Yeah, they're demanding at times, but more so, they're a lot of fun—and I love 'em!" Which teacher would you prefer for your child? Teacher A or teacher B? Joe Average or the Saint? What impressed me about the second teacher was not only her enthusiasm, but the multifaceted role she saw herself as having.

In a similar manner, how do you perceive your child? Would you characterize him or her as "about average" or as one who is (you choose): creative, competitive, methodical, perceptive, comical, serious, patient, a born actor, athletic, a tinkerer, musical—OK, I'll stop! Clearly, kids are more than just "good" or "bad" or "average." More importantly, kids are always in that constant "state of becoming." They're testing the waters, dreaming, learning, and playing with life. It's a tragedy, however, when we prematurely box (or frame) our perception of kids. Too many examples in history illustrate this misfortune. Listen to these descriptions from some teachers:

> *I am very concerned about her. She is bright and full of curiosity, but her interest in bugs and other crawling things, and her daredevil projects, are just not fitting for a young lady.*
>
> (about Amelia Earhart)

> *He is a unique member of the class. He is ten years old and only beginning to read and write. He is showing signs of improving, but you must not set your sights too high for him.*
>
> (about Woodrow Wilson)

> *He is a very poor student. He is mentally slow, unsociable, and is always daydreaming. He is spoiling it for the rest of the class. It would be in the best interests of all if her were removed from school at once.*
>
> (about Albert Einstein)

It's not only teachers. Louisa May Alcott's first editor swore that "she would never write anything for popular consumption." Walt Disney once got fired from one of his early employers since his boss felt that he "lacked imagination."

All of this suggests a word of caution. Don't be presumptuous, judgmental, or too limiting as to what your daughter or son can or cannot do, what they are or are not. Expanding your appreciation of them means going outside the box. Yes, reframing.

Career Profile: ***Tracy Groot, author of children's books***

At the age of eight, I wanted to be a writer. The most important thing my parents did was to supply me with books to read, including books from garage sales or flea markets or the library. Birthday and Christmas presents were always the holidays I loved most because I received books. My parents, however, had no interest in reading. By instinct, then, they encouraged my love of books.

This instinct, so tangibly expressed, became a form of validation for me. It made me promise to myself that someday I would dedicate my first book to them. I did.

How about the third message? It's found in that other point outside the box. It, too, offers a message about the possibilities that are available outside the box. Those possibilities are career opportunities. More precisely, they are career options that most of us rarely consider or are ignorant about.

You see, most of us devised our career options from our immediate environment: Mom & Dad, uncles & aunts, TV, stories, and even nursery rhymes. Some of us even had our career education taught to us through Parker Brother's board game called *Careers* where a player would select "Opportunity Cards" representing 24 careers. So much for the "world" of work. While rhymes and games are fictitious, they subtly confine our thinking. And too often, our real options. So, when you don't know what you don't know, you stay in the box.

This reality is so evident in our society. According to the Department of Labor, approximately 88% of working Americans are performing one of

133 occupations. The jobs include truck driver, attorneys, accountants, teachers, auto mechanic, etc. How about the remaining 12%? They're performing one of roughly 4000 other careers. While not to diminish the significance of any of those 133 careers, my suspicion is that those 4000 "other" careers offer tons more excitement and potential. For a reason that will be explained later, my contention is that those 12% of working Americans were willing to go outside the box. They were willing to explore and grab an opportunity that promised a lot. I suspect the Walt Disneys, Amelia Earharts, and Albert Einsteins of a different era were willing to do that. In the not-too-distant future, we all must face our willingness—or lack of—to reframe our thinking and consider the options. A number of futurists claim that by the year 2025, 80% of all jobs will be ones that are not in existence today.

To prepare for these many changes to the career landscape, we're going to have to re-examine those two outside dots. You see, there's a special connection between both of them. By leaving the box, we've suddenly expanded the universe of our understanding for both *ourselves* and our *options*. To illustrate this, take a drawing compass and place the point in the center dot of the original box with the pencil point on one of the four original corner points. Make a circle. Now draw a second circle by stretching the pencil point to one of imaginary points we created to complete the reframing exercise.

The comparison should be obvious and the message equally so. New and expanded perceptions yield many more never-thought-of, cutting edge, challenging, and more appropriate career options. Just ask Walt, Amelia, and Albert.

Leaving the box need not be a solo effort, however. This is all-the-more the case for our kids. Kids need someone to encourage them, introduce them, applaud them, love them. That someone is you, Mom or Dad. By sharing the experience of their growth, their imaginations, their victories, and their disasters, you help them realize their gifts. Essentially, you become a co-conspirator in enabling your child to realize their out-of-the box talents and those opportunities that are meant—uniquely intended—for them.

Admittedly, the co-conspirator uniform doesn't wear easily. There's that instinctive urge to protect our child, to do things for them, to secure things for them. Letting our children taste things for themselves has to be part of the equation, however. I guess it's simply letting them know that you can be both a close ally and a distant friend simultaneously. It's letting them realize that there's always a home base but there's so much more to experience beyond your four walls. It's living up to a parental creed which says that the "two best things we can give our kids are roots and wings."

Reframing. It's the first "R". Now, it's time for the second one.

The Second "R": Risking

A S.E.E.

Everybody has them. Some more than others. They're those special occasions that create in us the proverbial "indelible impression." For some people, they're incidents that alter your thinking, maybe even your life's direction. They're often known as S.E.E.'s—Significant Emotional Events. Let me tell you about one I had during the summer of '68.

It was following my junior year in high school. As the oldest of three boys, my parents felt that one more big summer trip remained for the family. So, we headed West. To the Tetons in Wyoming. If there ever is a spot where God vacations, it has to be there.

While the mountains themselves are the focal point of this national park, there is a small lake that serves as a tranquil contrast to the rugged peaks. It's called Jenny Lake. Adjacent to this lake, the mountains quickly rise almost by 90 degrees, creating a superlative setting for mountain climbers who want to hone their skills. It was while we were hiking in this area that I first noticed a group of climbers rappelling off a 120-foot cliff. I was immediately mesmerized. Yes, I was experiencing a S.E.E. Although our family's agenda wouldn't allow, I promised myself that I'd return someday, learn to mountain climb, and scale the Grand Teton itself. Seven years later, I did. Since then, I've been fortunate to climb other peaks.

For most people, mountain climbing is perceived as a sport reserved for the young, the agile, and the slightly eccentric. Yet, if properly learned, climbing is one of the safest sports. Serious climbers constantly test their equipment and climb with necessary back-up systems.

Still, there is an element that is particularly unique to climbing. A four-letter word. It's called "risk." That probably comes as no great surprise. And, it's our second "R" word. In a moment, more about how "risk" is a necessary component for successful career planning for our kids.

Undoubtedly, there are a host of activities much less risky than mountain climbing. Some people allege that merely driving out of the driveway is risky business (For parents of 16 year old drivers, this is particularly true!). Others view risk from a different perspective. At work, some individuals have to contend with a decision to risk their reputation for a decision, product, or policy they consider wrong or unethical.

I think you'd agree, however, that risk is most evident—and necessary—when people are kids. It's probably because just about everything is new, and in order to truly understand something for the first time, you've got to experiment—and risk. Remember riding without training wheels for the first time? Or, going to camp for a week without Mom or Dad? How about taking that first solo drive in the family car? And, do you recall the day you went off to college?

We all know kids—either our own or others—who are more or less risk-prone. My son, Taylor, is a prime example of one who doesn't know the meaning of risk, at least in a physical sense. As a nine year old, he couldn't get enough of "Der Stuck", the 110 feet, 70% degree water slide at Wet 'n Wild in Orlando, Florida. When he turned eleven, he learned to snow ski in a matter of minutes and was seemingly approaching Olympic speeds on the steepest runs by the end of his first day. For him, such stuff was a piece of cake. For us as his parents, it could easily be a cause of heart failure.

Yet, I've intentionally refrained from talking to him about the perceived risks involved with these activities. To do so might only squash an opportunity but, more importantly, diminish his genuine excitement for life in its many forms. He has nicely extended his "Just Do It" philosophy into theater, school, and part-time jobs. Yeah, I'm a pretty proud father.

As parents, we hope we've been there to encourage him plus our two daughters in most things. I suspect such encouragement is akin to "zapping", a term coined by Dr. Bill Byham in his best selling and appropriately titled book, *Zapp!*. The author uses this term for applications in business and educational settings by suggesting that people in supervisory positions are likely to be either "zapping" (empowering) or "sapping" (demeaning or discouraging) their employees. I suspect we've heard, witnessed, or experienced both sides. You're "zapped" when told "Good job!" "That's really helpful," or "Go ahead and give it a go." Conversely, you're "sapped" when hearing "That's lousy", "Why'd you ever do that!" or "We don't do it that way around here."

As parent/managers, we "zap" or "sap" our kids everyday, too. We convey this in what and how we say things. The smile, the frown, the arms folded, or the warm hug—all are messages of encouragement or discouragement, of love or emotional distance. Such messages create the necessary atmosphere for kids to experiment, test themselves, and risk.

Career Profile: **Pete Hoekstra, member of United State House of Representatives**

While my parents provided counsel and support, they also gave me freedom to explore and grow. This balance of direction and freedom taught me how to make my own decisions. My parents never monitored my perceived success or failure. Instead, they challenged me to do two things. They challenged me to be adventuresome and to take risks. As immigrants, they knew what it took to lay it all on the line; they had learned the value of risk taking.

Secondly, my parents challenged me to utilize every experience as a learning opportunity. They taught me that every event could be positive if I learned from it and used what I learned to inform future decisions.

Encouraging kids to risk is important for kids, particularly for those in the lower grades (Kindergarten through second grade). At this age, risking can be evident in a child's individual creativity. Unfortunately, a dramatic transformation occurs within a short two-year span. At age five, 90% of kids view themselves as "highly creative." Within two years, however, that figure drops to a paltry 10%. And only 2% of adults consider themselves as significantly creative. What happens to cause such a serious decline? In a word: criticism.

Prior to kindergarten, your preschooler is usually playing house, working on Lego projects, telling stories, drawing pictures, or constructing something—and doing so with a full measure of blessing and support. Starting with school, however, the dynamics are different. On a daily basis, kids are confronted by a jury of their peers (their classmates) with such indictments as "What is that?!" or "Yours isn't as good as mine." When encountering such comments, guess what happens to your son or daughter's self-esteem as well as their creativity?

As adults, we pretty much do the same to each other. When starting a new job, for instance, you'll frequently hear, "We don't do it that way around here." Another choice comment is "Why would you ever want to do that?" So, with comments and judgments like these, we tend to respond in one way: we go with the flow.

Going the way of the norm seems so un-American, doesn't it? There were and are simply millions of people from our history who took risks—big time risks—for new opportunities, new fortunes, new freedoms. They're immigrants. Their common experience has been one of fear, alienation, and uncertainty. Yet, the more compelling prospects of new employment and a better life for themselves and their families caused them to take the risks. Who would argue that the strength of our country comes in a large measure from such people?

In whatever form we wish to label it—risking, encouraging, challenging, or supporting—this willingness to tackle something is strengthened in community. Perhaps, you've heard the expression that "it takes an entire village to raise a single child." That community will include our churches, our schools, and most assuredly, our homes. In an era, however, when more and more kids are raised in single parent homes or in ones with no parents at all, doesn't this need for community become even more obvious, even more critical?

But, as in most instances, it needs to begin at home. With all the hats you must wear as a parent, none may be more important than that of instilling an attitude of risk-taking and independence within your children. Several longitudinal studies demonstrate a correlation between the degree that independence was fostered in the home and an ability to effectively act on one's own when an adult. Yeah, it's not easy to see your child occasionally get bumped, disappointed, or embarrassed. It's also just as simple to succumb to a child's natural protests, "I can't do that", "No Way!" or "That's too scary."

But push you must, because the life they live will eventually be their own.

> Come to the edge.
> "We can't. We're afraid."
> Come to the edge.
> "We can't. We'll fall."
> Come to the edge.
> Skeptically, they came.
> And he (she) pushed them.
> And they flew.

The Third "R": Romancing

They're in the stars, in the tea leaves, in Greek mythology, and even in Ann Landers. Some people swear by them. For many people, it's their daily dose along side their multiple vitamin. OK, what is it? It's their "horoscope" or their "fortune." And hey, if it's good enough for former first lady, Nancy Reagan, well.....

Personally, I guess I'm more than a little skeptical when it comes to my zodiac sign or what the fortune lady at the County Fair might offer me. I mean, after a while, all the predictions sound pretty hokey, far-fetched, or bizarre. More importantly, I think there's a higher Authority to draw upon when it comes to both my current situation and my future.

Yet, let me be totally honest. I have to confess to at least a little intrigue in a weird-shaped item found typically in mostly Chinese restaurants. Yes, I love fortune cookies. More precisely, I enjoy the anticipation of opening them. All of this is a preface to one particular fortune cookie that came my way in 1985.

On a particular evening in that year, my wife and I had a real yen (sorry) for some spicy Szechwan at our local Chinese restaurant. Going out and being away from the kids for a couple of hours gave us a chance to catch up and get re-acquainted. On our conversational agenda was a discussion about my career counseling activities. I shared my frustration in trying to get my clients to see the process as more enjoyable and inviting. Unfortunately, our conversation yielded nothing. By the time we were done with the main course, I found myself even more frustrated.

Thank goodness, a fortune cookie to the rescue!

My wife opened hers first, and while I can't recall her fortune, I'll always remember mine. It simply said, "Romance moves you in new directions." Was this another S.E.E. or what! Not quite, but it came pretty close.

And it did so because I suddenly sensed that the process of going after a new career should be romantic. Yes, *romantic*. Our third "R" word.

And why shouldn't it be romantic? After all, when else, besides when courting someone, are you likely to be so totally:

- Creative
- Energized
- Focused
- Excited
- Results-oriented
- Desirous
- Sensitive
- At your best?

Let me elaborate. In a true romance—we're talking the Romeo & Juliet types—lovers will do just about anything to be together, to get together.

You remember such times. You dreaded being away from each other. You thrived on the times where you were together. You did the most unusual things to impress each other and show your love. OK, true confessions. I gave my wife a rose each week from the time I first met her to the week that we were married. Once, we went out for double hot fudge sundaes six consecutive nights. And, I, Mr. Non-Poetic, wrote lines of verse that even rhymed—well, kind of rhymed.

When head-over-heels in love, one's charm is turned on 24 hours per day. You watch *what* you say and *how* you say it. And after leaving your date, you probably review every detail of the date. Undoubtedly, you recall saying something really stupid. So, upon getting home, you promptly get on the phone—and on your knees—to ask for forgiveness from your lover.

All of this points to a question. How should such a process be any different than pursuing a career or a specific occupation?

It shouldn't.

Initially, career planning may be more akin to "playing the field." That's, OK. It's a matter of checking things out. It's learning about things as your child learns about themselves. A kid needs particular assistance with this process. They need exposure to people, places, and things: computer software and animals in the zoo, skyscrapers and William Faulkner, playing fields and mission fields, politicians and X-ray technicians. If you don't do this with them, who will? And, please don't say "the schools." They do some but only some.

Introducing your child to something brand new is like meeting your date for the first time. It's all in the approach. What's wrong with demonstrating some kid-like anticipation as you drive into Disney World and the Magic Kingdom? Or, if you don't embellish that new spooky bedtime novel with all kinds of weird sounds of ghosts and goblins, your kids will probably think that all stories should be read just like listings in a phone book.

I genuinely struggle with people who don't possess or reflect much pizzazz in their life. Too often, such individuals are merely products of their own experience. That's unfortunate. What's even worse is that their experiences are then extended into how they interact with their kids. And so, the cycle repeats itself. That's even more disheartening. In such situations, both parents and kids miss out on the grand scheme of God's abundant creation. There's simply too much to be explored, felt, and embraced.

So, be juiced and energized for—and with—your kids. Chances are your enthusiasm for so much in life will rub off only to create a special dilemma for them. By engaging in so many ideas, people, issues, and professions, how will they decide what career to pursue? Reality suggests, however, that we, including kids, don't respond to everything with an equal amount of interest or disinterest, affection or disdain. If anything, there are nuances to every encounter, which, after a while, suggest a pattern and begin to yield a preference. Maybe even a passion. And when that happens, the romance *really* begins.

Well, there they are: the three "R's". Reframing, risking, romancing. The fundamentals. Key ingredients. Simple reminders. While they are meant to assist your child, they're equally, if not more, intended for you as a parent.

You begin with a paradigm shift (reframing) of how you evaluate and look at 1) your child and 2) the career planning and selection process. To really challenge those perceptions and to entertain a future where careers will be vastly different and work redefined, one must become a risk-taker. Yet the process of pursuing this new future is completely predicated on one's approach. In this regard, why not become a romantic about it all?

It's a choice you can offer your child. It's a blessing to bestow. It's a responsibility that comes with your calling as a parent. Enjoy it for your sake, for theirs, and for a larger Purpose.

Chapter II

Parenting 101: You Must Pass This Class First

The dateline is 8th grade. Your eighth grade. Or 10th grade. Or whatever grade you wish. You enter class, set your books and notebook on the desk, and Mrs. Davis, your less-than-favorite teacher, walks in. With a smirk. You immediately know what follows. They're 18 of the most dreaded words in the English language: " OK, class, put all your things underneath your desk and take out a sheet of paper. It's time for a pop quiz." You hate to admit it, but score one for the teacher. She caught you with your guard down. Perhaps, if you had been sick at home for the last three years, you could use that as an excuse not to take it. But, your options are zip. So, you gut it out and hope for the best.

Well, this is Professor de Roo, and yes, class, it's time to take out that out a sheet of paper for a pop quiz. Yeah, it's déjà vu all over again. This is a quiz, however, probably like no one you've ever taken before. This one covers you. As a parent. We're doing it to determine the effectiveness of your parenting role as a precursor to your role as your child's career facilitator. Putting together the parenting pieces will have a corresponding result in cultivating your child's career path. There's a strong parallel.

Nearly everything for you is supplied in the Appendix : the quiz (item B), the scoring key, and the rating explanation (item C). You just have to furnish the pencil. And the eraser.

Well, go to it, and I'll see you back here when you're done. Enjoy!

(When you're done with the quiz and you've scored it, please continue.)

OK, right now you're probably feeling either mighty good about yourself, pretty sorry for yourself and maybe your kids, or somewhere in between. Believe me, no guilt is intended or permitted as a result of this quiz. And, if we're totally honest about it, there simply isn't Mr. or Ms. Perfect Parent. We might think we know someone down the street or in our children's' school who *seems* to be the quintessential parent. What's more likely the case is that they're probably pretty strong in *one* or a *few* dimensions of parenting, but not the whole enchilada.

This brings me to a critical juncture in our discussion. As "the whole is the sum of its parts," the same is all-too-true when it comes to being a parent. There simply are certain parts of parenthood that come easily and naturally. Other ones simply don't. The reasons why-and-why-not are more appropriately detailed in other books by PhD's in Developmental Psychology. Overall, however, the parenting scale tips on the side of doing a pretty good job. Hopefully, the quiz pointed toward this conclusion for you as well as identifying and affirming specific areas within yourself.

But what are those "areas?" The remainder of this chapter will highlight those primary areas, traits, roles, and qualities we want to see in ourselves and promote within our kids—that is, if we really want to be serious about being an effective parent, particularly in the context of wanting to assist or kids with their career planning. Here they are:

- Instilling a spiritual and moral belief system
- Being a capable communicator
- Creating a safe, secure, and healthy environment
- Showing affection
- Frequently affirming and encouraging
- Intentionally exposing your children and yourself to various ideas, sights & sounds, people & places, and careers
- Having plenty of leisure, fun times, and traditions

- Instilling a sense of self-reliance, independence, and responsibility
- Giving the gift of time
- Assisting in identifying and celebrating your child's unique "imprint"
- Demonstrating patience and self-control
- Exercising discipline and fostering disciplines

A magical list? More precisely, an impossible wish list? Not at all. They're little more than some basic, common sense expectations. Do they require considerable time and effort? Will they require some self-sacrifice? That they will. Yet, each area can literally become a labor of love.

What follows is a brief explanation of each area with some "how-to's" attached. Adjacent to each subtitle is a list of the statements from the quiz that correspond to each area. As a suggestion, review the 40 statements, noting those items that you rated with a 5, 2, or 1. They'll affirm your "doing a job well done" or suggest an area that might need some attention.

1. Being a Capable Communicator (statements 5 & 36)

When I was a junior in college, a good friend and I went to his home in suburban Chicago for the weekend. Although I wouldn't openly admit to it at the time, I guess I simply desired a home environment—you know, home cooked meals, a clean bathroom, and a little motherly TLC. While I nicely got ample doses of all things during our visit, what I didn't predict was the mealtime routine. Everything was served buffet style at the counter and then we promptly gathered around the table to spend some time with, yes ladies and gentlemen, a portable TV. That's right, it was the literal version of the TV dinner. No conversation between family members, no casual conversation with the weekend guest (me). I mean we didn't even talk during commercials. It was anything but genuine family dialogue or basic hospitality.

OK, I think we'd all admit to an occasional TV dinner-type meal, such as during the Super Bowl or a major world event that's unfolding on TV. But, let's hope that such occasions are the exception to the rule.

Still, there's something unfortunate when recognizing that our *monologue* with the TV has replaced our *dialogue* between each other, particularly our family members. Statistics tell it all: the average person spends less than seven minutes in daily, one-on-one conversation with their spouse or their kids. The A.C. Nielsen Company (the TV ratings people) inform us that the average television set is on for an average of six hours each day. They suggest that TV viewing can either enhance or diminish the quality of family dialogue. Which one do you think it is? Just ask my college friend.

It would seem that if there's any single element that makes or breaks families, it's the issue of communication. That issue might be broken down to both the *time* and, more importantly, the *quality* of communication. In many ways, one might wonder whether true and meaningful dialogue at home has become a lost art form. I hope not..

It begins with the fundamentals. It begins with *listening*. When I was a kid, I can recall someone wiser than I saying, "The Lord gave us two ears and one mouth." How true. Maybe those two ears take double the effort, however. By that, I mean that listening—better yet, *active* listening—requires us to listen, process, and feedback.

There actually is such a method that works. In a process called "itemized response," a person periodically paraphrases the messages they think they're hearing. The paraphrase is followed by a comment that identifies a something of perceived value and, if appropriate, a remark that tactfully questions a part of the message. Here's an example between my daughter, Ingrid, and me after visiting my company's manufacturing facility:

Dad: Well, Ingrid, how'd you like the company?

Ingrid: I didn't! There's no way I'd ever work there.

Dad: Oh really. What makes you feel that way?

Ingrid: It was so noisy! My ears were ringing big time! In fact, they still are.

Dad: You know, I think the employees themselves would agree with you. That's why all the employees on the floor are required to wear earplugs. OK, so maybe things were kind of noisy. On the other hand, was there anything that you enjoyed about the day?

Ingrid: Yeah, the people were friendly. And, I enjoyed that CAD (computer-aided-design) station.

Dad: So, the employees were cool and you had fun seeing that demo on the CAD monitor. Maybe, someday, we could spend more time on the CAD equipment if you'd like.

Ingrid: OK, Dad. Maybe.

This type of give-and-take is an effort at achieving *understanding* and establishing *empathy.* What you didn't see at that short discourse between daughter and dad was perhaps the more significant part of the message: the non-verbal communication, an equally critical part of any message transmission and certainly something that makes or breaks a level of understanding and empathy.

Dr. Albert Mherabian, an expert in non-verbal communication, discovered that the emotional impact of a message is determined in the following manner:

- 7% of the time by the words we use
- 38% of the time by body language
- 55% of the time by facial gestures and the tone of our voice

Although my daughter, Ingrid, may not have the credentials of Dr. Mherabian, she seems to have a "sixth sense" about people. Believe me, Ingrid appears to be a master at sensing people's emotions merely by looking at them. She can conclude what type of day I've had within a matter of seconds after I return home from work—even without my stating a word. She does the same with strangers on the street or her teachers in the classroom.

Quite honestly, my wife and I have encouraged her to give some thought to counseling and social work where such an aptitude can be helpful. A word of advice for yourself. Next time be cognizant of the roll of your eyes, the furrow in your eyebrow, or a genuine smile. You've heard it before, but it's not what you say but *how* you say it.

At the same time, however, we cannot dismiss the importance of language. If you'll allow a bit of editorializing, one has to wonder about the direction of our language, specifically the quality of the words that we use. Increasingly, we seem to have lowered our language standards to the least common denominator. And, our language has become one characterized by four-letter words.

In many ways, we have prime time TV to blame. In a survey conducted by the weekly newspaper magazine, *USA Weekend,* 97% of respondents were very or somewhat concerned about vulgar language on TV. A high school principal, Jim Freese of Homestead High School in Ft. Wayne, Indiana, agrees. He says, "I'm seeing more instances of inappropriate language around school. It's part of the vocabulary, and often they don't think about some of the words, because they hear them so often on TV. It's a steady diet: Program after program has this inappropriate language." Isn't it time we elevate our language standards to some basic civility?

Finally, let's recognize that communication is a two-way street. So often, our dinner tables tend to be a division of the house. First, parents inquire about what happened at school. Consider yourself fortunate if you get a few words more than "Nothin'" or "Not much." After that brief agenda item, the parents move on to item B: a discussion about events at home or at work. But 99% of the time, that discussion is only between spouses. The kids are bored bystanders.

So, a suggestion. Why not allow the kids to be part of your "adult" conversation when appropriate. Let them be part of a problem-solving process. Get their perspective. Doing so, challenges their critical thinking and you just might come up with an even *better* solution. Also, encourage them to inquire about *your* day. It allows them to think outside of themselves and to see you as a person with activities and feelings, too. Rarely does a day go by when our kids don't inquire about our day. Thanks, guys!

In summary, communication is both a process and an art form. Equally important, it must be intentional and not occasional. In other words, it takes time—which is the subject of the next section.

"Communication" Reminders:

- Demonstrate "active" listening through paraphrasing.
- Do a "NVC" Test (Non-Verbal Communication).

2. The Gift of Time (statement # 13)

Seven minutes. 420 seconds. 0.0044% of a single day. No matter how you slice it, seven minutes per day is the average amount of time we give our kids. It's anything but a "gift" of time. Let's call it like it is: a major disappointment or, at worst, a cheap shot. It's more than a little disheartening when you realize that our kids experience more than 7 minutes of commercials in a single half-hour of their favorite sitcom.

You and I both know that it comes down to our daily priorities, right? After all, whose schedule doesn't have a mixture of breakfast meetings, a full day at work, a daily workout, 10 messages to return from the answering machine when you get home, a 45 minute commute, a dinner meeting, a church meeting, a PTO meeting, the golf league, or an evening class. Maybe, it's items A, B, & C—or worse yet, all of the above. But who's to blame you? Aren't we told that "life is for the living?" Furthermore, you don't want your career to be negatively affected or your life diminished if you don't participate in these things. Sure, the treadmill is going faster, but in the meantime, your son or daughter merely wants a story read to them.

So, then we tell ourselves that we may not give our kids "quantity time" but we certainly give them "quality time." By that we usually mean: a week at Disney World, a weekend hiking, a Sunday afternoon picnic at the beach, or an evening at the ballpark. And while not wanting to devalue these things, they really don't fully cut it. "Quality times" are really efforts at "fun times", but they too often disguise or shroud the everyday struggles, vulnerabilities, and neat things that kids experience—and want to tell you about. You see, kids live existentially. For them, each day—like today—is a "biggie." Relating to things next week, let alone next summer, is eons away. But again, if you're not around or "you don't have the time to talk right now," they're left wondering, guessing, and feeling pretty much alone.

There's someone who says all this much better than me. In fact, he *says* it in song. Although no longer alive, perhaps lyricist and singer Harry Chapin's most noted contribution was his ballad, *The Cat's in the Cradle.* Listen to the words and ponder your priorities.

The cat's in the cradle and the silver spoon,
Little boy blue and the man in the moon,
"When you coming home, Dad?"
"I don't know when. But we'll have a good time then, son.
You'll know we'll have a good time then."

"Timely" Reminders:

- What can you do—even today—to give each of your children more than 7 minutes of time?
- When one of your children wants to tell or ask you something, what generally is your demeanor?
- What are your real priorities? How can you realign your priorities to give your children more time?

3. Demonstrating Affection (statements 1, 12, 25, 35, & 39)

During my "formative" years (the ones the "experts" say are somewhere between 5 and 15; as though you stop forming, developing, or becoming after a decade and a half!), I lived in Emerson, New Jersey, a borough within 20 miles of Manhattan. While my current home is comprised primarily of people with Dutch blood, this community was 92% Italian. "Little Italy" might have been a more appropriate handle. And the phone book certainly testified to it; just about every name ended with a vowel. Great names like Sediducati, Gulino, and Peracci. If you've had the occasion to get to know Italians as I have, you know they are one EXPRESSIVE group of people. Not only are they vocally expressive, but they love to show it. Hugs, kisses, and more hugs are their standard *modus operandi.*

To this day, I think Italians know something that most of us non-Italians don't, namely the importance of showing and communicating affection. Isn't a basic need of all creatures in God's animal kingdom to know *and* feel love? One of the early studies that most Psych 101 students encounter is the research that demonstrated the intellectual and behavioral development of monkeys as reflected in those primates that had contact with some soft terrycloth versus those that didn't. Those chimps that were isolated from the touch of something resembling a mother's skin were severely retarded both intellectually and physically.

The same reality can be extended to *Homo Sapiens,* and particularly kids. A recent study suggested that a person needs 12 hugs each day. Not desires, wishes, or prefers. But *needs.* Perhaps, it's because a hug shows regard and affirmation. If anything, it tells another that they're *appreciated.*

And when it comes to expressing appreciation, don't think it's something reserved just for kids. Isn't ironic that the #1 desire for working folks is not a paycheck, great benefits, or 4 weeks of vacation, but some demonstration that they're appreciated? Don't get me wrong. I'm not suggesting that all CEO's start and end each day with a hug to each and every employee unless they're game for a litany of sexual harassment lawsuits. No way! Instead, a bunch of no-cost/ low-cost means can communicate appreciation just as effectively. Let's leave the hugging and kissing to families.

The importance of showing affection has been amply promoted by yet another Italian, Leo Buscaglia. In his book, *Born for Love,* he offers this, "In a study I did for an earlier book, *Loving Each Other,* respondents mentioned three qualities which they considered essential for happy, long-lasting relationships. It was rather surprising to find that affection (touching, holding, stroking) was named most important by the majority of them." It's been also learned that affection—the non-sexual touching type—is a valuable resource for physical and emotional well-being. And as Buscaglia points out, "It's free, needs no special equipment, and it's always available." I particularly like that "free" part.

Hey, how about giving someone a hug right now?

Affectionate Tips:

- When was the last time you showed some non-sexual affection to your spouse in the presence of your kids?
- How easy or difficult is it for you to show affection to your children, regardless of their age? How often do you display such affection: 12 times per day, once a day, once a week, rarely, never?
- Do you wish you were the person who invented the bumper sticker, asking, "Have you hugged your child today?"

4. Discipline and Disciplines (statements 6, 20, 27, & 32)

It's the classic confrontation: my 6-year-old niece, Blair, versus her 40-year-old Mom, my sister-in-law. The time: 8 p.m. The issue: bedtime. Mom says, "It's bedtime." Blair screams, "No way!" The tone of my niece's response tells me this isn't the first time this topic has been addressed. You've probably had these "discussions," too, so you already know the outcome. Mom is forced to get more than a little firm, carrying her up to bed as though carrying a wild alligator and finally "placing" her hand on her daughter's rear end. With this action, my niece breaks the sound barrier, but within minutes, a pleasant calm has been achieved—and welcomed by one and all.

Yes, with actions come consequences. Whether you call such consequences, "punishment," a "penalty," or a "correction," it comes down to the "d" word: "discipline." Those of us from the Dr. Spock era often thought that "discipline" was a dirty word. Yet, time, significant research, and even an admission from the famed child psychologist himself have come to see "discipline" from a more valued perspective.

Another famed psychologist, Dr. James Dobson, already touted such a perspective more than a generation ago. In his book, *Hide or Seek,* Dr. Dobson references a study by Stanley Coopersmith, associate professor of psychology at the University of California. In a longitudinal study involving 1,738 middle-class boys, beginning in preadolescence and following them through young adulthood, Dr. Coopersmith noted three important characteristics of those boys who eventually displayed the highest self-esteem. Besides 1) evidencing love and appreciation at home and 2) living in a home characterized by openness and democracy, it was discovered that 3) the parents of these boys had been significantly more strict in their approach to discipline. Conversely, the low-esteem group came from homes noted for their permissiveness.

Certainly, there's much that we hear everyday where physical discipline is actually a cover for child abuse. Zero tolerance is all anyone should have when learning about someone mistreating a child. It's also true that physical discipline is anything but effective for pre-adolescents or teenagers. Yet, appropriate discipline per the age of a child helps to create borders that reinforce what is right vs. wrong or proper vs. out-of-line.

Enough said about "discipline" when considered as a verb. Now a word about "disciplines" as someone like Benjamin Franklin meant it. I don't quite know whether Ben Franklin was a truly disciplined scholar, inventor, and statesman, but if he left anything as his legacy, it had to be the time management planner that bears his name. Actually, I doubt there's any real connection at all. Whether there is or isn't, I'll claim to be a victim. And if you aren't already a subscriber of his system or an electronic Palm Pilot, you'll be one soon.

The Franklin Planner system is based on some pretty simple principles. It actually prioritizes your life and has you plan your day, month, or year according to your priorities A, B, or C. The key is getting into the discipline of *using* the system and literally *keeping* it with you as kind of an alter ego. I've used it to remind me about maintaining my daily devotions, having a date night with my wife once every two weeks, and reading two novels each year. Would I probably do these things minus a planner? Maybe. Truth be known, probably not. If I had my druthers, I'd likely a) forget about, b) minimize, or c) defer or procrastinate most things. But then I'd also remember those words of wisdom: *Procrastination is opportunity's natural assassin.* Yes, I really do appreciate my planner.

So, disciplines are those usual-and-customary things we do to make things better. There also things that we remind our kids about like taking out the weekly garbage, brushing their teeth, or limiting the TV. There are also some positive disciplines that we hopefully teach our kids about like saving some of their money, giving a little money for someone less fortunate, exercise, and exercising the mind (homework) at a decent hour.

In summary, "disciplines" are synonymous with "habits" and someone much wiser than I once commented:

Sow a thought, reap an action;
Sow an action, reap a habit,
Sow a habit, reap a character;
Sow a character, reap a destiny.

Deciding on Discipline:

- How do you view "discipline?" To what degree, do your children see you as permissive or as a strict disciplinarian? Where is the happy medium and where are you in proximity to it?
- In what examples in your life, did you find personal discipline to be beneficial? What resulted from such a discipline or habit?
- In what ways or in what areas do you wish your children adhered to some personal disciplines? How can you partner with them in making those things happen?

5. Patience (statements 17, 21, 26, 28, & 40)

OK, here they are: I roll through stop signs. I hate waiting in lines at Disney World or at the supermarket. I simply don't understand why my wife is late getting ready <u>every</u> Sunday for church. I detest "waiting" rooms. I'm down on telephone recordings that say, "Your call will be handled in the order in which it was received." No, the good Lord did not bless me yet with the fruit of the spirit known as patience or self-control. Maybe, someday. I just wish He'd get around to doing it—and fast!

Fast, faster, and fastest. "The world belongs to the swift." "He who hesitates is lost." These things seem to have a distinctly Western cultural flavor about them, so maybe my impatience isn't so peculiar after all. Yet, is it right? What happened to taking time to smell the roses?

I suspect if there's anything that teaches patience to anyone, it's having kids. Yeah, it takes patience to tolerate your one year old crying at 4 a.m. or not giving the answers to your 7th grader's Algebra problems. And then there are *those* questions: the *why* questions. Someone once calculated that the average five year old will have asked one half million questions since their birth. Undoubtedly, a healthy portion of them are of the "why" variety. It takes patience to answer those questions, particularly when your child doesn't seem to get it the first time. So they ask again, and maybe again and…

Just remember, that patience, virtue, and kids go together.

<u>Points on Patience:</u>

- To what degree, would your closest friends consider you to be a patient person? How about your kids?
- How does patience play out in your daily life? In your career?
- Is "patience" a virtue in your family? How can it become even stronger?

6. Affirmation (statements 1, 14, 21, & 36)

Deviating from a family focus, there are a couple of #1 things that are uppermost in the minds of employers. The first #1 is with reference to the *most* important qualification that makes or breaks someone during the course of an interview. It's "attitude." Generally, it's either positive or negative. It can also be enthusiastic, engaging, cynical, or blasé. It's certainly not surprising that "attitude" ranks so high. After all, people respond and want to work with people who display the more positive side of attitude.

In terms of the foundations of differing attitudes, psychologists have much to offer. As suspected, it appears that much of our attitudes toward self and others are shaped during our formative years. Can you recall the earlier statistic about "creativity?" 90% of all pre-kindergarten children consider themselves as "highly creative". Then, school begins. This time, it's brother or sister, multiplied 30 times, that offer such critiques of schoolwork as "That's UGLY!" "What is that?!" or "You're stupid." Within a matter of 12 months, the statistics on those kids who still regard themselves as "highly creative" quickly plummets to a measly 10%. A total reversal.

Psychologists suggest that the affirming environment of the home, which applauded and encouraged creativity is suddenly and dramatically absent in kindergarten. Certainly, teachers are not to blame. Big-time competition and rivalries with other students is likely the cause.

Unfortunately, it's also found in other places. Statistics reveal that the ratio of "killer" phrases (basically, "no" statements) to positive statements are found in the following proportions:

Item	"No" statements/"Yes" statements
School	18:1
News	6:1
Home	2:1

All of this suggests that our attitudes, particularly the positive or negative ones, are often a product of our environment and the messages that are voiced and received. If those messages are powerful and frequent, we only tend to mirror them. They, in essence, become who we are. As a parent, there's message enough in this thought.

Now, a word about that other #1. If "attitude" is something an employer desires from a prospective employee, what does an employee, current or prospective, want from his or her employer? It's something even more important than a paycheck or job security. More important than a promotion, a company car, or a private parking space. It's another "A" word: "appreciation."

Career Profile: **Prescott Slee, Corporate Hospitality Services Director**

I grew up in the Bahama Islands, having moved there when I was four years old. My parents were what the hospitality industry calls "hotel people." Our accommodations were always in the hotels my parents managed.

During the twenty years I lived with my parents, I became more and more interested in the hospitality business. My parents never held me back from exploring the different facets of hotel management. When I was ten years old, I remember working with the bell captain, tagging luggage.

As the years went by, my parents recognized that I had a talent for this type of career. Both of them encouraged me. Their unconditional love was very important as I was leaving the nest. Their love, and the quality of people my parents were, greatly influenced me to follow in their footsteps.

Appreciation is basically a form of recognition, an acknowledgment—yes, an affirmation. Employees don't need a fat bonus to be so recognized. The occasional "Nice job, Suzanne" or "We couldn't have met the deadline without you, Gene" are especially valued and appreciated. And, they're either low cost or no cost. My former company utilized a form called "Feed My File" which allowed a person to acknowledge the simple or extraordinary efforts of another employee in written form. It just required checking one of eight categories, such as "Customer Service" and offering a one-liner about their effort. Then, they sent a copy to the person's team leader as well as forwarding a copy to their file in the Human Resources department.

This hunger for appreciation is universal, however, and particularly needed in the home. Offering some form of affirmation (a hug, a word of praise, a written sentiment) does wonders for a child's self-esteem and even more. In the book, *Your Child's Self-Esteem*, author Dorothy Corkille Briggs references this thought when mentioning that "The process of building self-esteem goes this way: a new reflection, a new experience, or a bit of new growth leads to a new success or failure, which in turns leads to a new or revised statement about the *self*. In this fashion, each person's self-concept usually evolves throughout his lifetime." It comes down to the interplay of affirmation and experience, which only result in new testing of aptitudes and, even more exciting, new discoveries.

Aiming for Affirmation

- What things can you do this day to praise more and reprimand less?
- To what degree, would you say that your family is a bunch of cheer-leaders?
- To what degree, do your children think that affirmation is only doled out when they achieve? Does this create excessive pressure for them?

7. **Gifts (statements 4, 12, & 18)**

When I was 7 years old, I discovered something beautiful along, of all places, the Pennsylvania Turnpike. It was a few days before Christmas and our family was en route to Michigan to celebrate the holidays with Grandma and Grandpa. My Dad decided to stop for a quick stop for gas at one of those service areas that materialize every 50 miles or so. Knowing that my Dad was kind of in a rush, he admonished us to stay in the car. Not even time for a bathroom break. Anyway, we all stayed in the car while the attendant pumped the gas and checked the oil. Snow had been falling lightly for a few hours, as I recall, which made all of us a little nervous through the hills of western Pennsylvania. While waiting, a snowflake parked itself on the windshield in perfect line with one of those towering lights that hover above the service areas. That powerful luminescence seemed to magnify that particular flake, exposing all the details of a flake in a way I had never witnessed before. Or since. It was simply a thing of splendor for even a 7-year-old boy. Somehow, I think the good Lord sensed my fascination because while the other flakes seemed to melt when hitting the warm glass, this one didn't.

I quickly called the rest of the family to check it out and it was then that either my mom or dad told me that no two snowflakes are the same. Now, how could they possibly know that? I guess I doubted that until a physicist friend of mine confirmed it some 30 years later. He indicated that the combination of water molecules, when crystallizing, is so complex and exponentially intricate that duplicate flakes are theoretically impossible. This scientist also hypothesized the same about people. Basically, no two of us are the same. No duplicate height and weight dimensions. No duplicate eye color. No duplicate personalities. No duplicate anything.

I think there's a reason for this. Each of us has been created with individuality, differing qualities, and yes, distinguishing gifts that make for nothing less than a fascinating world. Better yet, an ever-surprising world. And certainly, a world that needs to be celebrated due to its diversity.

Unfortunately, we rarely do this. By this I mean, that we box people in (remember the Nine Dots exercise?) to such an extent that we prevent or squelch the gifts that come with each of us. It's particularly disheartening when we do that to kids either at home or in school. Noted educator, Dr. Thomas Armstrong, in his book, *In Their Own Way,* states this, "If your child sticks out one iota from the norm—in other words, if your child shows his true individual nature—then there is always the danger that he will be discriminated against or stuck with some sort of label and treated like a category instead of a real human being."

Discriminated? Stuck? Who would want that for their child? If anything, a child's uniqueness—his or her gifts—should be treasured. Stay tuned on this very important theme. We'll talk in detail about the process of cultivating and identifying specific skills and gifts in Chapter V. In the meantime, some parting thoughts from Elizabeth O'Connor in *Eighth Day of Creation.* "Every child's life gives forth hints and signs of the way that it is to go. The parent that knows how to meditate stores away these hints and signs and ponders over them. We are to treasure the intimations of the future that the child gives to us so that, instead of unconsciously putting blocks in the way, we help that life to fulfill its destiny. This is not an easy way to follow. Instead of telling our children what they should do and become, we must be humble before their wisdom, believing that in them and not in us is the secret that they need to discover."

Going After Gifts:

- When was the last time you spent some time with each of your children for no other reason than to discern their mode of operation (how they do what they do)?
- Have you ever taken mental notes that identify what gifts they seemingly have based on how they play, perform, work, or interact with others? If you haven't done so, give yourself 15 minutes to list each child's gifts.
- How often, if at all, have you rushed to judgment, even if only slightly, in negatively labeling your child's intimations, intentions, or gifts?

8. The Home Environment (statements 2, 3, 6, 22, & 34)

I happen to live in the hub of the office furniture industry: western lower Michigan. No question about it, this area's predominant employers are the 50 plus companies that build the systems, chairs, desks, and component pieces that are found in most offices throughout the world. For six years, I was fortunate to work for one of these companies, Herman Miller. It was while working there that I became acquainted with the term, *ergonomics.* Basically, the word means the manner in which a person relates to a machine and vice versa. For obvious reasons, Herman Miller paid particular focus to how a worker uses, relates, or responds to their working environment. They pay attention to everything, ranging from the lumbar support in their chair to the ambient noise level in their immediate space. It really has become quite a science.

So, is there a comparable term to describe the relationship between one's *home* environment and one's *personality?* How about *homepersonomics*? OK, that's a stretch. Maybe another wordsmith can coin a more appropriate term.

Regardless, much that has been studied and said lends credence to the fact that our environment has much to do in determining who we are. We're not here to debate the ratio of nature vs. nurture. Suffice it to say, that much of one's environment, at least in our homes, is predicated on the quality of relationships and how that is expressed between family members, particularly between parent and child. Yet, there's no debating the plain fact that there are a number of environmental elements that can contribute to a child's quality of life. A few are worth commenting about.

Let's start with some basics. Basics, like clothing and shoes that are clean, warm, and in good condition. The principal of one of our local elementary schools asked for some assistance from a local business to make sure that each of her students came to school in the winter with mittens. No, the kids hadn't merely misplaced them; most of them came from homes where the family budget didn't include a line item on "mittens."

A similar necessity is living in homes and neighborhoods that are clean and safe. If a person doesn't feel safe and secure, any hope for other things is likely to be tough sledding. Neighborhood Watch programs, DARE (Drug Abuse Resistance Education), or Weed & Seed grants are efforts that unite neighborhoods, if not entire communities. Code compliance for homeowners and landlords is essential as well.

As long as we're being concerned with what's going on outside of our kid's well being, how about what's happening inside—more precisely, what goes into their bodies. Sometimes I wonder if junk food companies are a conglomeration of misplaced chemists who experiment with new-and-ever-changing ways to blend sugar, starch, carbohydrates, and a spoonful or two of caffeine. Such "foods" do wonders for one's glucose levels as well as the waistline. OK, every kid, big or small, is entitled to a handful of Skittles or Corn Nuts every so often. Just put it in balance with some fresh veggies and fruit. Doing so will keep one's system and psyche in running order.

Then, there's the matter of tools—and not the kind you might you might find on *Home Improvement.* The tool kit might include a well-lighted place where school assignments can be tackled. It should include a dictionary and a calculator and if the budget permits, a computer. The decor might include a combination of windows, color, photos, bulletin boards, furniture, or whatever else makes your home or your child's room inviting and stimulating. I once heard a speaker talk about their home having a CLC—a Creative Learning Center—where everything came together to provoke learning. What a concept!

Yet, if environmental science has taught us anything, it's that we all respond differently to various factors in our surroundings. Those responses will make real sense if they are consistent with our differing idiosyncrasies and preferences. In other words, the right place for one person may be a disaster for another. For most of us parents, an honest recognition of this (let alone an admission) is tantamount to heresy. This suggests that maybe my wife and I have to admit that our daughter Ingrid's consistently messy room is OK. As she often reminds us, "Hey, this place works for *me.*" The same can be said for the child who likes to study with double-digit decibels playing in the background. According to Professor Rita Dunn, an expert on learning preferences, "extroverted individuals learn better in a stimulating environment, while introverted persons prefer a quiet, calm environment with few distractions." Somehow, it's hard to fathom blaring tweeters and woofers as aiding my extroverted son in his academic environment. But hey, if it works, what can we say?

Certainly, all these things are mighty important. Suffice it to say, however, that they are pale substitutes for the "real things" that make or break one's home environment. Real things like love, hugs, appreciation, encouragement, and dynamic elements that make a house a home.

Engaging One's Environment

- Double check your child's basic requirements—good food, clothes, enough sleep, and a safe home—as fundamental preparation for growth and development.
- Rethink your purchasing priorities to ensure that your children have the right tools to learn and discover their world.
- Be flexible in your opinions about how your child's individual preferences translate into their own personal spaces. Remember: different strokes for different folks.

9. **Rituals, Leisure, and Laughs (statements 7, 8, 23, & 24)**

It's usually the late afternoon or early evening of December 22 or 23. At least, a few days before Christmas. We commence it with a mini-ceremony called "the lighting of the lanterns." What follows is the beginning of what we fondly regard as "Candlelight Night." For our immediate family and often with a portion of our extended family or some friends, we douse all the lights in our home and transform it into a Williamsburg-type dwelling that must have a zillion burning candles. OK, maybe a hundred, give or take. The evening typically includes hot dogs roasting in the fireplace, craft-making, a mini-concert of either piano, cello, or hammered dulcimer, and some robust caroling in the neighborhood. All in all, it's something of a really cool colonial Christmas. More precisely, it's become a much-looked-forward-to annual tradition for our family.

Traditions. Most of us have them to varying degrees. For some, it's a visit to the shore during second week of July. Others have annual family reunions. For years, my brother and I rekindle our love for the Scarlet &

Gray by attending the Michigan-Ohio State football game. Neither of us blinks an eye about the weather or how much we'll have to pay the scalpers. It's a tradition, and we just do it. They don't all have to be grand events either. Some have the tradition of going to the donut shop on Saturday morning. Maybe, it's Dad giving grace at noon on Sunday. Or perhaps, it's the whole family corralling around to watch their favorite weekly TV program.

Whatever the scope, traditions are a measure of cohesiveness. They serve a purpose as Dr. James Dobson suggests. "The great value of traditions is that they give a family a sense of identity, of belongingness. And everybody needs this in this harried day in which we live." Psychologist Claire Bernreuter, quoted in *Traits of a Healthy Family*, picks up on this theme when commenting, "Hope is what we need so badly, and hope is based in memory. Rituals do much to feed that hope through memory."

While it's easy to put "traditions" and "rituals" under the "Family Identity" category, I prefer to place them under the "Play & Good Times" heading. I think they are more appropriate there because they keep a sense of perspective about us and for us. They're departures from the routine. They usually permit us to "chill out." They often allow us to laugh a lot.

Each Christmastime, I, a.k.a. Santa Claus, send a note to my youngest brother, Dirk, informing him that once again, the fat man in the red suit will be bypassing his chimney due to a litany of bad things (each one is noted, of course) that he performed during the prior twelve months. I exploit all types of crazy and petty things about both of us. I know he is rolling on the floor by the time he's done reading it.

Traditions, laughter, and good times. Keep 'em coming!

Rituals, Legends & Laughter

- What rituals does your family have? Why are they important? Is it time to consider starting a new one—or simply starting one?

- When did you last have a belly-aching laugh? Who or what makes you laugh? Who does it to your kids? What do you see as the differences between as the sources between "good" laughter and "bad" laughter?
- When did your kids last see you laugh at yourself?

10. Exposure (statements 4, 15, & 31)

Twenty-two years old, a college senior attending his hometown college, and he's never been more than 25 miles from home. Hard to imagine. But it's true.

This describes a former client of mine (let's call him "Paul") who sought some confirmation of his career ambition of becoming a sales person. His sheltered existence was based on a family environment where members not only kept to themselves, but literally to their homes. It manifested itself in weak interpersonal skills, which I found to be ironic, considering his career interest. Paul's likely success in sales? Slim to none. So, we checked out more appropriate alternatives.

Throughout our discussions, the primary feeling I had for Paul was a genuine sense of sympathy. Here was a young man who had missed out on so many things: a major league baseball game, seeing a real mountain, riding a roller coaster, taking a trip on Amtrak or a flight to anywhere. And, it's not just seeing the sights. It's experiencing a group of people whose language or accents and traditions are different than his own.

Different than his own. Different than our own. It begins with venturing outside the box, even if that box has a width of 25 miles. It's called *exposure* and it critically important in the development of any child.

As you can imagine, exposure can run the gamut. It ranges from casually flipping through the pages of an encyclopedia to having your child join you at work for a day. It can be a trip to the Kennedy Space Center or hosting a foreign student for supper. It can be taking a tour at the Hershey's Chocolate Factory or scanning the night skies with a telescope.

To do this exposure thing right, however, a parent has to proceed carefully, patiently, deliberately, and creatively. As mom or dad, you should be using some creative effort in sketching out things to do or see or meeting people a little or a lot different than yourselves. Often, you'll have to remind yourself to do things in small or sharp contrast to how you were brought up. And you'll have to proceed in a fashion that takes you off the fast track for a while. Cynthia Tobias in *The Way They Learn* suggests this very fact when stating, "Perhaps, instead of spending so much time and effort trying to convince our children to move onto the path we've designed, we could encourage them to get to their destination by allowing a few minor detours. Who knows? We may even discover some places *we'd* like to travel off the beaten path!"

Merlin Whiteman, a fraternity brother of mine, was a man who lived for detours. Well, that's stretching it. While at Hope College, Merlin was one who was intentional about not taking the interstate back and forth between campus and his home in Columbus, Indiana. He did so because he found the nuances of each small town on the state routes much more fascinating than the exit signs on I-65. Something tells me he developed a better admiration for Middle America than I have because of this type of activity. He simply allowed himself a little bit of time for a lot more exposure.

A final thought. Parents offer exposure for a few reasons. One is an appreciation for the diversity of God's world. A second reason is to suggest and develop tolerance for those things and people that are distinct from us. And thirdly, exposure and experiences permit a child's gifts and talents to be compelled. They begin to surface. And with even more experiences, they begin to find expression.

Wrap this up with some lots of love, and your child is bound to make a mark!

The Essentials of Exposure

- What things were you exposed to or did you experience that influenced you in significant ways? How, if at all, did those things influence your career selection?
- How can you begin or continue to expose your children to differing people, sights, perspectives, and careers?
- If you're beginning to see some particular talents and learning styles of your children, how can you facilitate that even more?

11. Independence (statements 10, 12, 29, 30, & 33)

With the first child come lots of "firsts." The "firsts" I'm referring to for the moment are those of going away from home for the first time, even if it's just to the next-door neighbor friend's house. Or, maybe they're of the variety of the first date. I recall when Ingrid, our first child, was particularly anxious to pursue the most trepidacious of all firsts: the pursuit of her driver's license. For her, it was an event that couldn't come too soon. For her mother and me, we tried to postpone it a decade or two.

But who could blame her? We've all been there. That first driver's license is more than legal document. It's a badge of independence. Yes, it's one of those "taking on wings" things that us parents know to be true but hate to admit.

I guess we'd be more concerned if Ingrid was so anxious to get her license as a vicarious way of getting away from us. Knowing that is not the case, perhaps we can actually take it as a compliment, of sorts. I say this in the context of other things that suggest a mixture of being both a "home body" while simultaneously being comfortable as her own person and offering her own opinions.

As parents, we're in this ever-present state of holding on and letting go. Sure, we love our kids and would do anything for them. But do we smother them in the process? Or, do we too easily take on the bumps in the road that come with the territory of living? Family specialist Dolores

Curran poses some self-examining questions when asking, "Do we love our children enough to let them make mistakes and do the growing they need to do in order to leave us? Do we offer solutions or proposed rules that help our children, not to be better sons or daughters, but to live happier, more fulfilled adult lives?" In a similar vein, psychologist Howard Halpern advises "encouraging a child's independence at each fork in the road to adulthood rather than waiting until adulthood arrives before granting independence."

I can recall such a fork in the road as a nine or ten year old boy. Every Saturday night, we gathered in our station wagon for the eight-mile trip to Fair Lawn, New Jersey to pay homage to the Golden Arches. This was the era when there was no indoor seating. Everyone waited in line outdoors. On one Saturday night I joined my Dad at his side as we waited in line when, for an unexplainable reason at the time, he put the money in my hand and said, "You order tonight and bring the food back to the car." Instant panic. How could I do this? This meant recalling everyone's order and talking to an adult behind the counter. No way! I fussed and fumed. Even cried. Somehow, however, I did it. It's part of being pushed out of the nest.

Independence, however, is more than a growing-up thing. Its significance cannot be underscored, particularly in a society which, for the last forty years, has fostered a culture marked by dependencies. Too many persons have come to rely or depend on Uncle Sam for their food, clothing, shelter, and their destiny. What's to motivate anyone to do anything when you can get pretty much anything without much effort? The pattern of this type of living speaks more to a character flaw than anything. Yet, as noted author, Stephen R. Covey, comments, "True independence of character empowers us to act rather than be acted upon. It frees us from our dependence on circumstances and other people and is a worthy, liberating goal."

Worthy it is. An American tradition it is. Yet, there's more. We sum it up in the next dimension.

An Independent Examination

- Regardless of their age, what specific activities did you provide your child within the last month that caused them to think or act independently?
- When are you too independent with your child? When do you shelter them too much?
- When can independence negatively affect your or your child's ability to be a team player?

12. The Faith Factor (statements 9 & 16)

"Go West, middle-aged man!"

OK, so what if that quote from Horace Greeley is a little bit of a stretch. Maybe, it was his middle-aged cousin who wanted to quote his more famous relative. Whoever Mr. Greeley or his cousin intended, I know those words compel this middle-aged person every so often.

They certainly did for my family and me during the summer of '95. That particular summer, our family spent a week at a dude ranch of sorts at a place called Trail West. TW is a family camp run by Young Life, a fine Christian organization for high school and college students. In between the rodeo, the jeep hikes, the utterly fantastic wrangler breakfast, and the white water rafting was a message. Sometimes, it was spoken. Often, I just sensed it. The message for the week—and really for a lifetime—was a simple one: if you think you can do it on your own, forget it. There's Someone who is willing and able to assume the load.

Wait a minute! A page earlier, there's stuff about the virtues of independence, particularly when it comes to advocating self-confidence and individual resourcefulness in making things happen in an increasingly tough, dog-eat-dog world. The problem with "independence" is that when taken to its logical extreme one eventually gets so caught up with no one but himself or herself. It becomes the ultimate act in selfishness.

Stephen Covey, in his landmark book, *The 7 Habits of Highly Effective People,* talks about the preferred continuum of our development, beginning with our dependent demeanor but through maturity hopefully a direction toward independence. Yet, according to Covey, there's something more. He suggests that "as we become independent—proactive, centered in correct principles, value driven and able to organize and execute priorities in our life with integrity—we then can choose to become interdependent—capable of building rich, enduring, highly productive relationships with other people." Toward the summation of his book, Covey readily admits that the center of his principles is God, the Creator and Father of us all.

Unfortunately, ours seems to be "The Age of Self-Help Books" that panders one quick fix after another. Instead of rock-solid answers, such books often leave lots of empty questions—and wallets—in the process, including those of young people. For adolescents, in particular, theirs is an age of introspection. The media increasingly promotes the power of "Me" for answers. Psychologist Dr. Robert Coles of Harvard University says, "Many of the kids I looked at don't have faith. They have lost everything except preoccupation with themselves. That's a problem."

Perhaps, they should have been talking with those families who have a strong religious core. George Gallup in a survey on "parenting" discovered that 63% of responding parents, claiming a "very religious" upbringing, experienced stronger family relationships with their own children. Furthermore, they felt it enabled their own children to better handle their own problems in a significant way.

If, however, we pursue going to church or having mealtime devotions as a way to improve our family, to gain better friends, or to jump start our career, we've missed the point. Our relationship with God is a response of obedience. God merely seeks to be in a loving relationship with his creation in a way that is truly "up close and personal." Such a relationship weaves itself through everything we are or hope to be as persons, as parents.

Questions of Faith

- How is a spiritual dimension evident in your life? In your family's life?
- When do you bring job or career-related issues to prayer or a discussion with others who share a personal faith in God?
- How often do you pray for career direction for your children?

Chapter III

The "Ex Files"

It's been "one of those days." You've had your share and so have I. It was the kind of day when I had a zillion things going on. By 10 p.m., I'm ready to zone out. My choices are either the bed or the couch by the TV. On this particular day, I opt for the latter. Flipping channels, I come upon the beginning of one of those no-brainer, beachside shows. Although such shows aren't prime Emmy candidates for the quality of their script writing or much of anything else, this particular show—more precisely, the opening dialogue—grabs my attention.

The two main characters, one a female FBI agent (let's call her "Sandy") and the other, a thirty-something life guard (his name is "Jeff"), inquire of each other as to how they got into their chosen careers. Let's pick up the dialogue. Jeff to Sandy, "How'd you ever decide to become a FBI agent?" Sandy pauses, reflecting, "When I was in fourth grade, our family took a trip to Washington, DC, and while we were there, we took a tour of the FBI Headquarters. Everything I saw there convinced me—right then and there—that's what I wanted to be." Jeff is impressed. "Wow, that's cool!" Then, Sandy inquires the same of Jeff. He offers, "Our family lived just a couple of miles from the beach here in Long Beach. For me, it just became a daily thing to come to the beach. I became friends with the lifeguards, and just like you, I was hooked. I mean, what could be better than the beach, the babes, and the surf?" Get what I mean by "quality" script writing?

Even if the dialogue isn't award-winning material, most persons you know can replicate the child-age experiences of this TV scene in "real life" situations. Maybe, even yourself. It comes as no shock that most kids are pretty impressionable. One event, one person, or one place can brand a permanent impression into us. And sometimes, those impressions materialize into life-long professions.

Fred Mester, a circuit court judge in Michigan traces his interest in law from the time his family took trips to Springfield, Illinois, where they visited the historical sites of a famed attorney—an attorney who gained even greater prominence as the 16th President of the United States. Henri Nouwen, perhaps one of the most insightful theologians of the twentieth century, traces his leanings toward the priesthood from a maternal grandmother who created a "mini-chapel" in her attic. Phil Groenhoef, a tremendously successful tool and die maker, cites the many times his father took him into his workplace where he witnessed the almost artistic finesse of a metal part being formed out of raw steel. Cokie Roberts, the acclaimed news analyst, cites the journalist background of her mother combined with her father's political career as the launch pad for her interest in reporting.

What the stories of Fred, Henri, Phil, and Cokie point to is a paradox of sorts. On the one hand, you just never know what turns someone on. But, at the same time, be assured, that *something* or *someone* will. And with all that the world offers, both good and bad, that opportunity for your child might just be determined by what *you* do for and with them. It comes down to something pretty basic. Something we'll call *The Ex Files.* Through them, your kids will learn about themselves, you'll discern some special patterns within them, and the combination of them could be the basis for their eventual career selection. Considering this, their importance should be obvious.

The *Ex Files* begin by resurrecting an age-old debate, otherwise known as "Nature vs. Nurture." It's a dichotomy that has puzzled psychologists, geneticists, and everyday Moms and Dads. There's no question that our genetic code determines a generally predictable level of intelligence or even a propensity toward certain fields. Take the Bach clan, as in "Johann

Sebastian," for instance. For several consecutive generations, the world has enjoyed the fruits of these musical geniuses. A study of this extended family reveals intellectual levels, which are almost off the charts

Perhaps it's not true about you, but most of us have not been imparted with the intelligence of the Bach's. It's simply not in the genes. So, we do the best with what we got. And what we have are mostly those things that we see, touch, taste, and encounter. It's what we experience. This is the "nurture" part. If we subscribe to this, doesn't it stands to reason that a person's true colors will become either strikingly real or dully shaded by the **breadth** and **depth** of various experiences in one's life? Put another way, there may be a correlation between our "calling" as persons and those things we encountered in our lives—whether such ideas, events, or experiences were real or imagined, visualized or fantasized. When considering this idea, the career implications are downright awesome.

Contemporary author and futurist, Faith Popcorn, references this notion in *Clicking,* her book about emerging trends. She quotes the following poem from *The Tao of Pooh,*

How can you get very far,
If you don't know Who you are?
How can you do what you ought,
If you don't know What you've got?
And if you don't know Which to do
Of all the things in front of you,
Then what you'll have when you are through
Is just a mess without a clue
Of all the best that can come true
If you know What and Which and Who.

There are lots of thoughts and key lines in this poem, but the one that grabs me is *of all the things in front of you.*

Invariably, that line conjures up all kinds of images of a huge smorgasbord, the kind that you see at a Sunday brunch at a nice restaurant. When such an opportunity comes my way, I create a sampler plate. A little of just about everything. Except lima beans, of course. I guess I developed this practice after succumbing to some advice from my mom and dad.

Like most kids at a buffet, I initially limited myself to the four primary food groups: French fries, pizza, chocolate cake, and chocolate milk. Not my parents, however. They fashioned a plate for themselves with everything *but* my choices, and it was always accompanied by the comment, "You don't know what you're missing." So, I experimented. I tried some twice-baked potatoes, glazed carrots, and a mint parfait—and I enjoyed them! Suddenly, I was a food connoisseur at age 10. Soon, I relished the opportunity to test out new and different foods.

You get the picture. The poem's line, *Of all that is in front of you,* speaks to the array of choices, options, and opportunities that is spread out in front of each one of us. Taking advantage of those options, however, involves a bit of intrigue, investigative savvy, and risk. Having kids, in particular, do things *intriguing* or *risky* runs counter to what most parents think they should be for their children: protector and guardian. That's OK, up to a point. Yet, if you don't engage in things different, creative, or intriguing you can't access *The Ex Files.*

Career Profile: **Robert Gamblin, manufacturer of artist's oil colors**

My parents gave me an excellent education and direction in what was right and what was not. But they made no attempt to influence, recognize, or foster any special interest or talent I might have.

I have chosen to do the opposite with my son, facilitating his interests and giving him exposure to things that might spark his interest. Since he is 17, it is too early to judge whether my approach will help him.

So, what are the *Ex Files,* or at least one of the *files?* Well, we've hinted already about the need to introduce or to acquaint your child with the smorgasbord of the things in this world. Let's call this by its particular file name. It's the *Exposure* file, the first of the two *Ex Files.*

To get a more accurate handle on what is meant on this file, we'll have to call on Mr. Webster. There are upwards to 10 definitions for the noun, "exposure," with two, in particular, that have relevancy. The first, I guess, is partially appropriate when it cites "exposure" as *the act of disclosure, as of something private or secret.* Certainly, some things we expose our kids to might be regarded as semi-secret. But exposing your kids to the sap running in March or shadowing a nurse in the ER isn't secret stuff.

It's the second definition that lands some punch. This explanation suggests that exposure is *to subject, as to the action of something, such as exposing a photographic plate to light.* Wow! Think of that split-second when a negative in the darkroom is suddenly exposed to light. That's not just chemistry. And it's more than literally a picture-in-the-making. It's a revelation! And in the case of your kids, exposing them to something for the first time can be their personal awareness coming to light. And you made it happen.

Fortunately, you don't have to own all the photographer's gear, equipment, and chemicals to access the *Exposure* File. It's mostly a no-cost, low-cost program. Basically, it's creating opportunities for your child to see, touch, taste, and hear what's around them. The menu might include both familiar and unfamiliar sights, sounds, textures, and people. It could involve hands-on things, physical challenges, or intellectual insights. It's uncovering things for the first time, and if some things click, fantastic! But if they don't, that's OK. The ultimate objective is not arriving at final decisions or charting a life-long vocation. The purpose is merely to check out some things.

Successfully using the *Exposure* file requires a few key ingredients: being creative and a little funky, applying some basic discipline, taking advantage of the serendipitous, not spending tons of money, and approaching things slightly different from how you've always done them.

Here are a few quick instructions on each item, starting with the latter. Approach situations with an *open mind.* Undoubtedly, it's an easy invitation to introduce your kids to the same things in the identical manner that your parents did to you. So why should you be any different? If you're like most of us, you'll probably acquaint your kids to *your* personal interests. That's understandable. It's what you know best. Remember TV's, Tim "The Tool Man" Taylor? He was a prime example of this. Tim would be the first to admit that his world centered on three things: great tools, the Detroit Lions, and vintage cars. Nothing gave Tim more pleasure than seeing his boys getting turned onto any one of the same. Thank goodness for the Tim's next-door neighbor, Wilson, who offered a measure of worldliness and wisdom. A true reality check.

As with Tim, however, it's tough for most of us to know what to introduce our children to that exists outside our comfort zone. Sometimes visiting the Science Center in the "Big City" or riding bikes to the Nature Center on the other side of town may be first-time encounters for us, too. And, that can be a little disconcerting. A quick solution is in the *presentation.*.

Near our home in Michigan is a well-known restaurant called, *The Piper.* It is situated in an idyllic setting along the shore of Lake Macatawa, an inland lake that is connected via a channel to Lake Michigan less than a half mile away. The adjacent tree-covered dunes create a hilly effect that strikingly resembles the San Francisco Bay area. Only a scaled-down version. Not only is the setting simply gorgeous but the food is both casual yet cosmopolitan. Bar none, it's our favorite restaurant.

Whenever we dine there, we're in for two experiences, actually two special presentations. Although menus are offered, we're finessed with an oral presentation courtesy of the waiter or waitress. He or she entices us with a tempting description of the spices, special marinade, or unusual cooking technique. The second presentation is on the plate as the food is served. The chef has to be a kissin' cousin of Martha Stewart because the food is always artistically displayed. Especially the desserts. Such a display gives credence to a food critic's mantra that "at least half of the enjoyment of a good meal is not in its taste but in its presentation."

Presentation is equally true when anticipating or sharing an *Exposure* file with your kids. Maybe, even more so. The tone of your voice, the enthusiasm on your face, and the spirit you exude makes all the difference. If you're excited to see the leopards in the zoo on Saturday, guess who else will be? If you're pumped to view this month's full moon through a telescope, guess who will want to view it first? If you're willing to offer a bribe to your daughter so that you can be her substitute on the class trip to Washington, DC, guess who will be all the more psyched to go? In other words, surround any new activity for your child with some excitement and intrigue. Better yet, TONS of excitement and intrigue. Yeah, be a kid again. Get turned on again! Get juiced! What a huge difference it makes to your child to know that *your* interest is genuine and FUN. Really anticipating an upcoming activity can make all the difference between something super or something mediocre. It's all in the presentation.

Another part of the process is *seizing the moment.* I can recall a time when our family was en route to Colorado for a family vacation. Driving for nearly 14 hours, we finally arrived at our halfway destination: Omaha, Nebraska. After settling into the hotel and grabbing a much-needed splash in the pool, we decided to have supper in downtown Omaha. OK, let's be honest. We weren't particularly hopeful when it came to restaurants in downtown Omaha. So, we were more than pleasantly surprised when, by luck, we happened upon a renovated part of old Omaha, complete with cobblestone roads and sidewalks, street vendors, inviting restaurants with utterly fantastic aromas, and ornate Victorian architecture. The place was wall-to-wall with people. Everyone was having a blast. Within no time, we got caught up with it, too. More importantly, our kids saw some neat things that they hadn't encountered before. So did Mom and Dad.

Grabbing hold of these *carpe diem* (Seize the Day!) experiences is something not only to celebrate but to be appreciated. The following words say it much better:

Yesterday is history
Tomorrow is a mystery
Today is a gift
That's why we call it "The Present."

As suggested, the *Exposure* file also requires some *discipline.* Translated that means doing and seeing some different things on a regular basis. It may simply involve checking out the weekly Town Calendar in the Sunday paper and then taking advantage of some local activities or events. It can be as simple as making monthly resolutions that ask "What can we do with our kids that we've never done before? What can we show our children that would be totally new and different?"

Doing so will often involve a change of routine, and this isn't always easy. For instance, it might suggest that you deviate from your usual vacation at the *same* beach in the *same* cottage on the *same* week of July. Maybe this year, you and your family check out the blooming rhododendrons in April by hiking a section of the Appalachian Trail. Or, maybe the family takes on a *real* challenge by serving on a mission project on the south side of Chicago.

It doesn't have to be so dramatic either. Locating a spot near an airport runway and seeing jets take off and landing can be pretty cool. Something else that kids of all ages never tire of is browsing a bookstore. And then something that requires little imagination but yields big dividends is story-telling in bed. As a child, my favorite pastime was lying next to my grandpa and hearing stories that exposed me to distant lands, some true, most imaginary.

So, what types of other things—specific things—can you expose your child to? Or putting it another way, what can we find in the *Exposure* file? The answer exists in your imagination, your own experiences, plus some guesswork about the future. It also means being intentional and gutsy about checking out things beyond your perceptions, stereotypes, and traditions. What follows on the next few pages are some ideas to get you going. This list is anything but complete. Just a start. Embrace some of them. Initiate some of your own. And, "just do it."

<u>Key:</u>
P = Pre-kindergarten
L = Lower elementary grades
U = Upper elementary grades
M = Middle school age
S = Senior high school age
A = Any age

1. Surf the Internet (A)
2. Subscribe to a magazine of the child's choice (L, U, M, S)
3. Play the "I Saw" game in which the parent asks the child at the end of the day, "What did you see today that was special or different from something that you never really saw before?" (L, U)
4. Window shop (P, L, U)
5. Stop by historical markers along the road and talk about the person whom the marker commemorates (A)
6. Take nature walks (P, L, U)
7. Visit a Children's Museum (P, L, U)
8. Visit a Planetarium (P, L, U)
9. Talk to grandparents and great-grandparents about life when they were kids (A)
10. Read biographies (U, M, S)
11. Check out and monitor the construction of a building project. If possible, talk to the architect, engineers, or construction manager (U, M, S)
12. Become a pen pal (U, M, S)
13. Attend plays, concerts, operas, and musical events (M, S)
14. Participate in hands-on creative activities that are sponsored by your community's Arts Council or Association (P, L, U)
15. Enroll your child in a "leisure" type hobby class (M, S)
16. Visit and simply browse through a bookstore (A)

17. Purchase a disposable camera for your child and have them take pictures of anything. Yes, anything! (L, U, M, S)
18. Host a foreign student from an area high school or college for a home-cooked meal (M, S)
19. Purchase or borrow a telescope and check out the solar system (L, U, M, S)
20. Visit an art gallery (U, M, S)
21. Ask your child about a favorite product, store, or entertainment place. Then, buy one share of stock and have them monitor its performance (M, S)
22. Subscribe to the *Occupational Outlook Quarterly,* a publication about specific careers and job trends (S)
23. Check out the booths at a local convention or professional meeting (A)
24. Visit historical sites and attractions, particularly those that feature "living history" (L, U, M, S)
25. Eat a meal at an authentic ethnic restaurant (A)
26. Read a good book with your child (P, L, U)
27. Attend "Story Time" at your local library (P, L)
28. Purchase an encyclopedia and encourage your child to browse through it (P, L, U, M)
29. Take a tour of your community's architecture (M, S)
30. Visit a national, state, county, or city park (A)
31. Take a tour of an area manufacturing facility or in one that links to your child's interest (U, M)
32. Visit a TV or radio studio (U, M, S)
33. View educational TV program, e.g., National Geographic's *Discovery* (U, M, S)
34. Attend "Open Houses" sponsored by local businesses (M, S)
35. Travel, travel, travel! (domestic or international) (A)
36. Visit your state's capitol building (M, S)
37. Visit a fish hatchery (L, U, M, S)

38. Participate in constructing a "Habitat for Humanity" House (M, S)
39. Participate in an "Earth Day" project, e.g., cleaning up a littered river bank (M, S)
40. Visit a zoo (P, L, U, M)
41. Collect things, ranging from coins to car parts, from baseball cards to butterflies (L, U, M)
42. Visit a hospital (U, M, S)
43. Attend a political rally or convention (M, S)
44. Plant and tend a garden (M, S)
45. Create greeting cards (L, U, M, S)
46. Regularly check out the "Community Calendar" in your newspaper or local cable TV channel. Then, attend an event or activity of interest for your child. (A)
47. Create your own computer program (U, M, S)
48. Visit an aircraft controller in the airport tower (M, S)
49. Spend a day on a working farm (U, M)
50. Attend a church service or a synagogue that is different from your own (A)
51. Attend a symphony (U, M, S)
52. Observe a repairperson, a carpenter, or a plumber who comes to your home to do a project (U, M, S)
53. Be responsible for a family pet (L, U, M, S)
54. Attend an Air Show (A)
55. Visit the Humane Society or a Veterinarian's office (U, M, S)
56. Tour a submarine, aircraft carrier, or other Navy vessel (L, U, M, S)
57. Visit a Space Museum (L, U, M)
58. Visit an airport (P, L, U)
59. Visit your state representative, congressman's or senator's office (U, M, S)
60. Read the daily newspaper and watch the news (L, U, M, S)
61. Attend a City Council meeting (M, S)
62. Attend a School Board meeting (M, S)

63. Visit a fire station (P, L, U)
64. Write a government official, expressing an opinion (L, U, M, S)
65. Set up a bird feeder and/or a bird house or some type of feeding stations for other animals (L, U, M)
66. Visit a nuclear reactor or a power plant (U, M, S)
67. Visit a Native American burial site or historic pictographs (U, M, S)
68. Visit and shop at an antique shop (U, M, S)
69. Design and make something out of Play-Doh (P, L)
70. Create and present a puppet show (L, U, M, S)
71. Visit and attend your State Fair or a County Fair (A)
72. Build and shoot off a model rocket (U, M)
73. Browse your local library (A)
74. Identify and conduct career information interviews with persons who are minorities (M, S)
75. Identify and conduct career interviews with persons in non-traditional roles (M, S)
76. Participate in a school's "Wonderful Wednesday" or "Fantastic February" program that sets aside some time (half-hour at noon or after school) to develop a particular skill (ethnic cooking, magic, cartooning, quilting, karate, etc.) (L, U, M)
77. Learn about different careers as it pertains to current topics being taught in schools. Encourage your teachers to host, in class, parents whose career reflects the material being taught, e.g., an environmental engineer speaks about ecology. (L, U, M, S)
78. Post a world map or purchase a globe and identify places as they're mentioned in the news. (L, U, M)
79. Attend Open Houses of new plants or additions to facilities (U, M, S)
80. Attend a Book Fair (L, U, M)
81 Check out garage sales (L, U, M)
82. Visit specialty shops, e.g., nature/ecology, pets, computers, plants, ethnic items, hiking/camping, etc., (L, U, M, S)

83. Develop a card catalog system either manually or on a PC that catalogs all their books or those of your family (M, S)
84. Go camping (L, U, M, S)
85. Attend and/or participate in a historical re-enactment, e.g., a Renaissance Faire, Civil War or Revolutionary War battle, etc. (U, M, S)
86. Participate in school field trips, either the 1-day or extended (3-14 days) variety (L, U, M, S)
87. Regularly review the "Computer" section in your newspaper that highlights new websites. (definitely worth checking out!) (L, U, M, S)
88. Imagine with your child by painting "talking" pictures with them. Play with them by posing a lot of "imagine how" questions, such as "Imagine how it would be to be:
    1) a TV reporter
    2) a minister
    3) an astronaut
    4) an archeologist
    5) a geologist
    6) a web page designer
    (P, L, U)
89. Serve as student representative on a Community Foundation or United Way (organization that dispenses funds for local projects or social service agencies) (S)
90. Participate in a Summer Reading program at the local library (P, L, U)
91. Read award-winning books, such as ones that receive the *Caldecott Medal for Illustration* and the *Newberry Medal for Writing* (P, L, U)
92. Visit different types of post-secondary institutions within a 100-mile radius of home. Check out the differences between small, medium, and large institutions; public and private; classical liberal arts and more vocationally-oriented. Nearly each institution has a

special institute, museum, collection, laboratory, or arts facility that is renowned and open to the public. (M, S)

93. Develop a family tree and note the vocation of each family member. Check for patterns of careers, if any, from generation to generation. (U, M, S)

So, what about the other *Ex File?* Well, pardon the bias, but the *Exposure* file is a sample, a teaser, just an hors d'oeuvre. The main entree—the real meat—is found in what Webster characterizes as a *being affected, positively or negatively, by what one meets to such a degree that one undergoes a change.* His word? *Experience.* It's our other *Ex file.* Consider it a type of *encounter*—as in the "up-close-and-personal" kind. This is the type of happening that demands some involvement. But, it's more than that. Whether it's small or significant, it requires a level of commitment. A way of comparing both *Ex files* is seeing *exposure* as window-shopping and *experience* as weighing the options and making the purchase.

Like *exposure,* the *experience* file has its own set of criteria. They include involvement, reflection, and response. A few words on each—and I mean only a few words since *experience* is getting out there and doing something. Just reading about it doesn't count.

First, *involvement.* If there's probably one word that has been overly used, abused, and misused, it's this word. Yet, the *Experience* file can't ignore it. Involvemen*t* is something that requires lots of who you are—literally. Like your delicate nerve endings. Like those taste buds on your tongue. And, most certainly, those dendrites in your brain. In other words, it captures just about every part of who you are. Involvement isn't a distance thing either. More precisely, it's getting involved in the thick of something. *Experience* demands a whole lot more. Paul Mosser, a former working colleague of mine, always used to quip, saying "Learn it, love it, live it."

Experience is also something that loses its true impact unless *reflected* upon. In T.S. Eliot's literary piece, *The Dry Salvages,"* he writes, "We had the experience but missed the meaning." Whether the experience was good or bad, we gain some wisdom when we're willing to ponder the experience. And that usually requires some good, honest, hard self-reflection. Rather than immediately moving into the next experience, a few quick but thought-provoking questions can help in this regard. Questions such as: What just happened here? What impressed you? What skills did you use?

OK, waxing philosophical and asking these questions by a 9 year old who just happened to experience operating a lemonade stand for a couple of hours isn't too likely. At least, not by any nine year old that I've met lately. (Maybe, the same could be said for most 39 year olds.) As a parent, the reflection process for your child should begin with you. And hey, it's simple and painless. It need not be more than 1) asking them how they felt about the experience and 2) affirming them for something you saw them do. Sometimes, you'll hear some truly amazing insights. Other times, not much. Don't force it. Eventually, however, your occasional prompts will be internalized to the point where it might become second nature to them. It's what educators label as "critical analysis" or "independent judgment." It's what a parent calls "growing up." And when it happens, give yourself some credit. Nice job!

And there's one more dimension to experiencing something: a *response.* After all, for every cause there's an effect. For every stimulus, a response. So, it reasons that everything we experience or engage in has a likely consequence. Well, sort of. Sometimes, our kids do something but when it's all said and done, about the only thing they want to do is yawn. For a number of reasons, it just didn't do it to them. And that's OK. It probably didn't resonate with who you are.

On the other hand, sometimes an experience that really clicks leads to bigger and better things. For instance, there's Mandy, a 16-year-old high school sophomore who, with some prompting from her parents, successfully created and marketed some really impressive graphic designs as part of a Junior Achievement project. A friend of her father's saw her work and now has commissioned her to develop a new logo for his young company. One activity spawned another and *voila!*

Responses to an experience shouldn't be just the purview of your child's. Your eagerness to hear about your child's *ex file* experience is something your child needs to know. For instance, whenever your son sees the first evidence of the seeds he planted, whom does he want to tell first? When your daughter has designed a perfect urban plan on her *Sims City* software, whom does she want to first explain it to? When your child kicks that first goal in their soccer game, who do they search the crowd to share the moment? For a child, nothing sounds sweeter than a parent's "Super!", "Great Job!" or "I'm proud of you." Nothing is more important, more necessary, and more appreciated than your words of affirmation.

Not only does your affirmation convey a degree of interest, but it also serves as permission to move forward. Your appreciation and interest provide some valued encouragement to stretch, to experiment, to excel a little more the next time. One of the products of such support is further interest in a topic or subject. For example, your daughter's seed experiment project just might lead to an interest in genetics. Or your son's *PowerPoint* presentation leads an interest in electronic marketing. Remember Mandy? Her parents' acknowledgment of her artistic talent resulted in her successfully creating some impressive graphic designs.

The other product of a parent's reassurance is *skill development.* When one experience is followed by another and yet another and your child is intimately involved in the activity, you begin to see something: improvement. It's evident whether your child is kicking a soccer ball, performing in a school play, or building a go-kart. True, some kids show improvement quicker than others. Much of it depends on your child's natural intelligence. Regardless of how quickly the improvement materializes, it causes a special reaction for parents: pride.

Such things are the sum-and-substance of the *Ex Files.* Here are a few examples where some initial ex*posure* sparked an interest which led to some neat ex*periences* which led to......well, you'll find out.

Scenario #1: Mom takes Lori to the local bookstore.

Lori flips through a book of pictures by Ansel Adams, the famed photographer/naturalist.

Mom buys the book for Lori's birthday.

Lori starts taking photographs in abundance with the family camera.

Since Lori is monopolizing the camera, parents decide to buy Lori a 35mm with a telephoto lens for Christmas. Lori goes bananas!

By now, Lori is in high school and she decides to join a local Photographers' Club where she picks up tips from other photographers.

Lori displays some of her pictures in a photo contest and wins 2nd Place; (so what if the prize is only 5 rolls of film!)

Lori gets a part-time job in a local camera shop.

A local professional photographer with a regional reputation frequents the shop and is immediately impressed by her expertise. He wonders if she has a portfolio since he has an opening for an assistant. Lori hustles like mad to pull together a portfolio.

Her portfolio more than impresses the photographer. She gets the job and her hopes of becoming a professional photographer are realized.

Scenario #2: An item in the Tanis family's church bulletin asks for host families for a group of visiting Japanese students who are visiting their community over an upcoming weekend. The Tanis family talks it over and agrees to entertain a student.

The Tanis family spreads out the royal carpet for Kutiyaka who they quickly nickname, "Katie." Both Katie and the

Tanis family learn tons about each other's culture and respective countries. Emily, the Tanis' 8th grader, is particularly fascinated with Katie and what she has learned in just a weekend.

Although the weekend comes to a happy-yet-teary conclusion, the relationship has not and Katie and Emily become immediate pen pals.

In 9th grade, Emily must write a paper on a foreign country and her selection in a no-brainer: Japan. She studies much, gets some great info from Katie via e-mail, and even secures some Japanese art courtesy of a former Japanese missionary who now resides in their town.

Following 2 years of active e-mails, Katie invites Emily to visit her during the summer. Emily is ecstatic and agrees to go for 2 weeks in July. To say that those 2 weeks were a learning experience would be an understatement.

In college, Emily develops a double major in Japanese and International Studies. Part of her studies involves an internship. With Katie's assistance, Emily gets a position in Tokyo's International Trade Center.

Emily can't get enough education, so she pursues a Master's degree in Cross-cultural Relations at the American University in Washington.

Upon graduation, Emily is an attractive candidate for the State Department. Her first assignment is with the US Consultant Office in Nagasaki.

Scenario #3: Jason, a high school sophomore, has no specific plans beyond high school. He's a good student yet his school days mostly involve little more than trekking from one hallway to another.

Patrolling the high school's hallways is Robert Boswell, a.k.a. "Officer Bob," who the school principal has secured to "keep the peace."

Jason and Officer Bob strike up a friendship, which begins with learning how Officer Bob got into law enforcement.

Bob offers Jason an opportunity to join other officers in the local Police Department on weekend patrols. Jason accepts.

Officer Bob is asked by his Sergeant to identify some potential undercover teenagers who might be involved in a "sting" operation to nab local liquor stores, which might be selling beer to underage teens.

Officer Bob immediately thinks of Jason and privately asks him.

Jason jumps at the chance. His first taste at undercover work goes so well, Jason is repeatedly asked to participate in similar stings.

Jason volunteers to serve on a federally funded "Weed & Seed" program in their community whose purpose is to identify trouble makers as well as foster supportive services, e.g. Big Brother.

By the time, Jason is ready to graduate from high school, he has already applied and been accepted into an Associates degree curriculum at the nearby community college in Criminal Justice. While Jason's dad had high hopes of having him follow his footsteps as a toolmaker, he totally supports Jason's wishes.

To top things off, Jason receives a scholarship from the local Police Officers' Guild. For Jason, life is good!

Three simple scenarios. These three could be multiplied a zillion times over in terms of how careers happen. Each of them points to the subtle yet potent influence of the *Ex Files.* Breaking down each scenario by each *File* demonstrates how.

Scenario:	*Exposure:*	*Experience:*
# 1: Lori	Trip to bookstore.	Takes tons of pictures. Receives book by Ansel Adams. Joins local Photographers' Club. Secures a part-time job at the camera shop.
# 2: Emily	Tanis family hosts Katie, a Japanese student for a weekend.	2 super weeks visiting Katie in Japan. Works as an intern at the International Trade Center in Tokyo. Learns much through study. Corresponds with Katie via E-mail. Views and obtains some Japanese art.
# 3: Jason	Converses with Officer Bob.	Serves as an undercover "sting" volunteer. Volunteers in the community's "Weed & Seed" program.

In each case, the *Exposure* file ignited the interest, but it was the *Experience* file that clinched it. The following list offers an array of experiences that just might do both. Fortunately, they don't require a six-figure bank account, trips to the Great Wall of China, or a 21-day Outward Bound trek to the Yukon. Yet, if you agree that "There's no substitute for experience," it's definitely worth the effort to get your child involved in as many experiences as possible.

Check out these options on the next few pages within the *Experience* file for some possible ideas:

<u>Key:</u>

P = Pre-kindergarten
L = Lower elementary grades
U = Upper elementary grades
M = Middle school age
S = Senior high school age
A = Any age

1. Shadow someone in the work place (M, S)
2. Conduct an information interview at the person's workplace. (M, S)
3. Participate in "Take Your Child to Work" Day (U, M)
4. Participate in Junior Achievement (S)
5. Set up a road-side stand, e.g., lemonade stand (L, U)
6. Sell something door-to-door (U, M)
7. Teach or tutor another child (S)
8. Participate in an apprenticeship program (S)
9. Get a part-time job (S)
10. Participate in a co-op program (S)
11. Join a sports team in a sport of their choice (L,U, M, S)
12. Encourage your child to participate in extra-curricular activities (L, U, M, S)
13. Attend Summer Camp (U, M)
14. Attend a specialty summer camp program (S)
15. Research, present, and participate in a Science Fair (M, S)
16. If your school has one, participate in a "Career Academy" which, in some cases, is a year long, in-depth exposure to various careers (S)
17. Take an "Alternative Vacation" in which your family substitutes a typical vacation for an extensive service project-type one. (M, S)
18. Host a foreign student for a semester (M, S)
19. Study a foreign language (A)

20. Accompany a police officer or an Emergency Medical Technician (EMT) for a shift (S)
21. Keep a diary (U, M, S)
22. Serve as an intern for a governmental official or a political party (S)
23. Audition and perform a role in a theatrical production for a school production, local civic theater, or Children's theater (L, U, M, S)
24. Participate in a youth group's mission trip (M, S)
25. Work as a student reporter for a local newspaper or the student paper (M, S)
26. Shadow a reporter for a full or partial day (M, S)
27. Participate in an "Adopt-A-Mile" program to pick up trash (U, M, S)
28. Work with your child in developing a budget with their allowance (U, M, S)
29. Use and own a ATM Card (Automatic Teller Machine) (U, M, S)
30. Conduct an "Information Interview" with someone at their workplace (M, S)
31. Plant dune grass as part of an environmental project (U, M, S)
32. Participate in planning or participating in a local parade (M, S)
33. Serve as a volunteer at the local hospital (S)
34. Become a school crossing guard (U)
35. Open up and monitor a checking or savings account (L, U, M, S)
36. Design, build, and race a soapbox derby and sew your clothes and fashions (M, S)
37. Imagine and create your own jewelry (M, S)
38. Design and create your own clothes and fashions (M, S)
39. Produce a video as entertainment or a documentary (M, S)
40. Conduct an "oral history" on someone or something by recording on audio tape (M, S)
41. Volunteer in an archeological dig on a local excavation (S)
42. Write or edit a Neighborhood Newsletter (M, S)
43. Troubleshoot and repair a problem with an appliance, an electronic item, a bike, or a car (M, S)

44. Participate and attend a school's "Market Day" where students promote and sell products they made or manufactured as part of a school project (L, U, M)
45. Collect autographs/signatures of famous people by sending them individualized letters. Learn about each person prior to sending them your letter. (U, M, S)
46. Serve on a high school's "Teen Court" where student violations, ranging from parking offenses to carrying firearms on school grounds, are dealt with. Students serve in real-life roles as a jurist, prosecuting or defense attorney, judge, or bailiff. Decisions are binding and cannot be appealed. (S)
47. Work as an interpreter for a social service agency. (S)
48. Volunteer as a Junior Docent at an area museum. (S)
49. Serve as a campaign volunteer for a political candidate. (S)
50. Run for office. Develop a campaign, seek volunteers, give speeches, etc. for any office in a club, student council, class office, or actual civic office (check out age requirements for this). (U, M, S)
51. After your child reads a book (a novel or non-fiction) that made an impact on him/her, visit some of the sites referenced in the book and talk to people who now live in those places and get their perspective on the people, places, and events that happened there. (A)
52. Volunteer in a community service project or a social service function (U, M, S)

Whether it's Mandy, Albert Einstein, or Helen Keller, a special adult—in many cases, a parent—took advantage of the *ex files* and what a difference it made. String together enough of these *ex files* for your own child and a career interest begins to take form. Guaranteed.

But, just doing the *ex files* isn't enough. They require some probing, some analysis, and some dissection—which is what you'll do in the next chapter. This type of investigative analysis will yield your child's particular *imprint*, which is fundamental in selecting the appropriate careers. If you need a minute to grab a magnifying glass and a sharp pencil, go ahead. You'll need 'em.

Chapter IV

What's Your Child's "Imprint?"

The streets are cluttered with all kinds of busy people on this particular morning. Foreigners from Cairo, Ephesus, and Baghdad exchange greetings in their native tongue and barter with the locals in this thriving metropolis, a.k.a. the city of Babylon. The scene is replete with customers negotiating the best prices on cinnamon, brass, papyrus, and pigeons. It resembles a modern day Farmers' Market, but the calendar says 434 B.C.

One of the more colorful vendors, Paktar, is speaking feverishly with Milenius, a veteran spice distributor from the island of Crete. A casual observer doesn't know if their conversation is more of an argument or a spirited discussion about an impending business transaction. It soon becomes a real test of wills and, as usual, the focus of their dialogue has to do with a selling price. The matter at hand is a fairly large quantity of sheep and goats' hair, two highly regarded commodities from Crete.

By now, they have become a genuine "side show," attracting quite a gathering. Their animations soon mellow, however, as the two sparring foes break out in smiles. A deal has been struck. All that remains are a couple of notations on their version of a "buy/sell" agreement: a one foot square, four pound clay tablet which requires their "fingerprint signatures." To perform this ritual, they pour about a tablespoon of water on the lower right hand corner of the tablet, causing it to become almost putty-like. Delicately, both gentlemen position their right-hand thumbs on the soft stuff. They do so with such precision so that the ridges of their fingertips can be easily distinguishable. With this "signing," the transaction is final. Paktar and Milenius leave as happy campers.

The focus of this story shouldn't be so much a description of early commerce as it should be about "fingerprints." That's right, those tree-like rings at the ends of your digits. Perhaps, the ancient Babylonians comprehended the distinctiveness of individual fingerprints long before it was used in science. It wasn't until 2200 years later that Sir Francis Galton, a noted British anthropologist, began observations that led to the publication in 1892 of his appropriately named book, *Finger Prints.* His studies established the individuality and permanence of fingerprints. Somehow, Paktar and Milenius recognized this fact all along.

When one thinks about the true individuality of a fingerprint among the billions of people on this planet, it has to be more than a scientific curiosity. It's simply amazing. Our own special fingerprint is indeed something that each of us can claim. It sets us apart from every other human. It's a genetic "brand" which knows no predecessor or successor. No wonder detectives rely so heavily on them when investigating crimes.

However, there's another fingerprint-like uniqueness about each of us that goes beyond biology. It's the source of our passions. It's our "claim to fame" and it, too, is as individual as a thumbprint. In a word, it's our *gifts.* And when it comes right down to it, anything that has any connection to who we are and what we're meant to be starts with an identification of our God-given gifts.

Such a recognition lies outside of conventional wisdom or academic thought. You see, "gifts" sounds too Pollyanna or lacking credibility when part of a job-related discussion about skills, competencies, promotions, or job titles. For instance, when did you ever fill out an employment application and see the statement, "Please list your gifts in the section below." Skills maybe, but gifts no.

More recently, however, people and organizations are looking beyond a list of skills by inquiring about where your *real* expertise is or what your *true* competencies are. I guess this is a masked effort at trying to identify a person's gifts without being so direct. I became introduced to this emphasis on "competencies" when taking a graduate course in Industrial Psychology. I recall the prof stating that the usual sequence for becoming "competent" is a four step one, beginning with discerning one's 1) *aptitude.* If developed, the aptitude evolves into 2) an *ability.* Then, when refining one's abilities, you are hopefully becoming 3) *skilled.* And finally, if that is perfected, one arrives at the summit, otherwise known as 4) *competent.*

Well, maybe.

You see, I contend there's a difference between being *falsely* competent and being *genuinely* competent. In other words, the real stuff. I'm sure there are many of us who know of someone—maybe, even you—who has taken scores of college courses and training programs. Or perhaps, such persons will show you a resume that lists some pretty impressive positions at some equally prestigious organizations. These people might be solidly convincing on paper, but if they lack the *passion* that must be part and parcel of their competencies, of what real impact will they have?

As a business coach and consultant, I often probe a person's genuine competencies through interviewing. Regardless of a candidate's level or rank, one of the questions I invariably ask is, "When do you best *shine*? When are you at your best, and you and everyone else knows it?" 99% of the time that question evokes more positive emotions than any other question I'll ever ask. And, it's not surprising. You see, *shining* is natural. Sure, it takes lots of elbow grease to become really good and competent, but the inspiration is innate. It's innate because it's *stamped* or *imprinted* on us. Like a fingerprint.

It's also a God-given gift. It's the source by which one derives their true and genuine competence. Eventually, that source will transform itself into *passion* and if passion is blended with skill, watch out! Think of the implications if organizations were able to attract and cultivate their employees' *genuine* competencies, their real gifts. Wall Street would be setting records each day—guaranteed!

All of this is meant as a preface to some questions within your role as Mom or Dad. From your perspective, what is your child's special *imprint?* When does your daughter or son *shine?* What have they been *gifted* with? Where are their true and genuine preferences? What separates their profile from that of others? Equally important, how does one link those gifts and preferences with career fields or specific job titles? Where will their gifts and competencies lead them?

You're already ahead of me. Actually, some career theorists have been ahead of both you and me in developing a process to answer these questions. With permission from them, you're going to have the opportunity to assume the mind and manner of your child in doing the same profiling assessments and career interest inventories.

But not quite yet.

Before we do some of the "Check the boxes with a #2 pencil" activities, I'm going to ask you to postpone the test-taking assignment. Trust me, we'll do such a test, but not until Chapter V. For the moment, let's have you switch roles from that of test-taker to that of an historian, psychologist, researcher, and biographer. The subject of your investigation or analysis is your child. While any one of these experts relies heavily on empirical data, they need to go beyond the numbers by sensing things within themselves. Call it intuition or learning through observation, but a keen researcher will, over time, perceptively know what makes their topic tick. The same principle applies to a parent's knowledge of their child, particularly when it comes to recognizing your child's *imprint.* Nella Barkley, author of *How to Help Your Child Land the Right Job,* suggests an approach that utilizes your understanding of your child. She contends that "the best way to learn about what makes your client (daughter or son) tick is through her life history. Hiding in her childhood, school days, various work and volunteer experiences, hobbies, and leisure time is abundant information about her skills, values, interests, ambitions, and the environment in which she flourishes. By tapping into these experiences, you will help her answer the question, 'Who am I?'"

I'll admit that asking the "Who am I?" question is pretty heavy stuff. Maybe, it conjures up a self-searching pilgrim on a Tibetan mountaintop. Perhaps, it takes you back to your freshman year in college when such a question was given on the first day of Philosophy 101. Let's not make it so complicated. Instead, let's simply rephrase it by means of a few related questions in an effort to uncover and identify your child's *imprint.* Again, we're doing this as a necessary prerequisite to linking *who* your child is with *what* might be appropriate options for them in their career.

Career Profile: **Judeth Javorek, Chief Executive Officer of a hospital**

When I was 18, having graduated from high school, I moved to Sydney, Australia in search of myself. I found challenge and novelty as a "go-go" dancer while I went to school, taking very liberal, liberal arts. This is definitely not what a mother wants from a daughter from an excellent Catholic school background. My mother took matters in her own hands, made an appointment from me with the matron at the local hospital, and found myself on the train and sitting in the nursing school the very next Monday. Despite being described throughout my training as having "more heart than head," I did graduate. And so the story began!

My father (my soul mate and friend) spent most of his life bemused at the ability of his wife to positively manipulate the destinies of her seven offspring who became, respectively:

A fireman
An artist
A model
A fashion designer
An architect
Another fireman

On the next few pages, you'll be asked a series of questions that probe your child's experiences, the tone and substance of their words, plus your perceptions of your daughter or son. As you respond to each question, think about your *child's* mindset, *his* or *her* experiences, and *his* or *her* words. Not *yours,* or what you want them to be. Too often, we answer questions with what we think is the ideal response but not necessarily the plain truth. Honesty is indeed the best policy, particularly when it comes to your child and their future. Next, take a long-term, comprehensive view in answering each question. It's an easy invitation to magnify one particular situation that happened just yesterday which may or may not be consistent with how they typically behave. Look at the whole enchilada.

One more instruction. Answering test-like questions, particularly the mini-essay type, isn't usually easy, let alone enjoyable. I mean the True/False-type tests are a whole lot easier, right? It helps to simply remember whom you're doing this for. So, go to it! And we'll briefly discuss a way to interpret your responses at the end.

Questions to identify your child's *Imprint:*

1. What kinds of things (activities, situations, objects, interaction with others, etc.) just seem to come naturally to him/her? When do they really *shine*?
2. What things does he/she most enjoy in their leisure time?
3. If applicable, what type of work experiences or jobs has he/she enjoyed? What made it so? What particularly motivated him/her in those jobs? On the other hand, what work experiences or jobs were less-than-satisfying and why?
4. What people (friends, relatives, sports heroes, entertainers, political figures, persons in the news, teachers, historical individuals, etc.) does he/she most admire? What is it about these people (skills, traits, characteristics, career choice, values) that makes them special to your child?

(For the next 11 questions, check the item in each set that your child would likely prefer. If you can't decide between two, check both. You'll use this information in the next chapter)

5. Which is most typical of the topics for conversation that are started by your son or daughter?
   A. Things in books or magazines
   B. The logic of computer games
   C. Things they may have made or want to make
   D. Music or musicians
   E. Sports or fitness
   F. How to get along with other people
   G. How to understand things about themselves and how they solve their own problems
   H. Things related to nature or the outdoors
   I. Why bad things happen to good people or the reverse

6. Your son or daughter wins a gift certificate to select one book or magazine from each of the following sets of books. Which category are they most likely to select from?
   A. Harry Potter, Lord of the Rings, or a collection of mystery and horror stories
   B. Mind Games, How to Design Your Own Games, How to Win at Computer Games
   C. Art for Everyone, Crafts on a Budget
   D. Famous Rock & Rollers, How to Play Your Instrument Better, Lyrics of Pop Tunes
   E. Sports Heroes, Fitness Today, How to Create a Beautiful Body
   F. *Psychology Today,* Guide to Popularity, Why Your Friends Act the Way They Do
   G. How to Understand Your Feelings, Are You Normal?, How to Understand Your Dreams
   H. *Outdoors*, *Backpacker*, Animal Adventure, *National Geographic*

I. Why Wars Happen, Is Justice a Myth?, Why Are Some People Poor?

7. The school suddenly offers free tutoring (once each week) in one of the following areas. Which one is your son/daughter most likely to select for themselves?
A. Improving creative writing skills
B. Math, physics, or chemistry
C. Arts or crafts
D. Music
E. Sport or dance
F. Understanding people from other cultures or applied psychology
G. Career alternatives and life planning
H. Biology, animal husbandry, or natural science
I. Social justice or Faith in Action

8. It's the first day back in school after the summer break. Their first homework assignment is an essay on "What I Did During My Summer Vacation." Your child selects which of the following topics:
A. My Review of the Best Novel of All Time
B. Ten Easy Steps to Build a Paper Airplane (or a project of their choosing)
C. The Paintings of Claude Monet
D. "Rock Music Rocks"
E. What Makes Tiger Woods So Good
F. The Incident That Changed My Life
G. The Formula for Cutting Your Homework in Half
H. 30 Insects I Found in my Backyard
I. What I Did to 'Think Globally and Act Locally'

9. Which would your child's favorite elementary teacher praise your child for?
   A. Reading or writing skills
   B. Solving math problems
   C. Art or crafts ideas
   D. Music ability or music appreciation
   E. Sports or dance
   F. Working well with others
   G. Understanding their own strengths and weaknesses
   H. Fondness for animals, nature, or the environment
   I. Concern for how people are treated

10. What subjects does your child prefer or are most enjoyed by him/her?
    A. English or a foreign language
    B. Math or physical science
    C. Arts, crafts, including woodworking, sculpture, etc.
    D. Music or the history of music or musicians
    E. Sports, physical education, or dance
    F. History, sociology, or the studies of other cultures
    G. Personal psychology
    H. Biology, geology, or earth science
    I. Studies of different religions or beliefs

11. When you ask your son/daughter about the teacher(s) they learn the most from, which of the following are most likely to be highlighted?
    A. When they describe things, I can really see what they are talking about
    B. They outline and simplify things. Their descriptions help guide me through the steps

C. They use lots of pictures, graphs, and objects so I can see what they are talking about
D. They are easy to listen to, not boring or dull
E. They allow us to touch things, move about, build, or use our eye/hand coordination
F. Give us a chance to work in groups or pairs
G. Encourage us to use our own initiative or ideas
H. Often use examples from nature, the environment, or the natural world
I. Make us examine and challenge our personal beliefs and values

12. Your child's class will soon go on a field trip. If your child had the opportunity to sit next to a new teacher on the bus, what type of teacher would your child prefer?
A. A talker
B. A cool, logical teacher
C. A teacher really into art, photography, or design
D. A music teacher
E. A sports fanatic
F. A teacher who enjoys talking about celebrities
G. A teacher who is interested in your child's life story
H. A teacher who loves the great outdoors
I. Someone who loves to talk about creating justice and fairness in the world

13. Which of the following is most likely to annoy or frustrate your son/daughter?
A. A torn or abused book or magazine
B. Disruption of patterns, order, or logic
C. Colors, patterns, or designs that clash
D. A scratch or small mark on a music CD

E. Malfunction on a piece of sporting, dance, or fitness equipment
F. Inability to meet the needs of others
G. Failure to achieve or satisfy their own personal standards or goals
H. Abuse of animals or trash in the environment
I. Prejudice or stereotyping or another social injustice

14. Which of the following sounds most like your son/daughter?
A. Using colorful words or expressions when talking
B. Figuring out math problems in their head
C. Assembling things, such as electronic equipment, a bike, or a model, with relative ease
D. Always humming or singing a tune
E. Always outdoors, playing some kind of sport
F. Being the first to initiate or organize a game, an event, or a conversation
G. Create a check list for themselves
H. Always fascinated by something they saw in nature
I. Asks a host of "why" questions

15. Your child has excelled beyond expectations and is ready to enter Excel University. Like most major universities, EU has a number of different colleges that comprise the campus. Which of EU's respective colleges is your son/daughter likely to enroll in:
A. College of Literature & Journalism
B. College of Math & Technology
C. College of Industrial & Machine Application
D. College of Musicology
E. College of Physical Education & Athletics
F. College of Communication & Human Services
G. College of Psychology

H. College of Natural & Physical Sciences
I. College of Philosophy & Religious Studies

Nice job! After going at those fifteen questions, it's definitely time for a break. But don't take too long because while you're on a roll, it'd be good to begin to check out what this all means.

To begin with, go back over and read what you've written. You're welcome to edit a few things or add some others. Then take one more gander. Look for the themes. As you review your responses, what common perceptions, consistent messages and unique images are you discerning about your child that makes them different than anyone who ever was or will be? Hopefully, these 15 questions and your perceptions will enable you to better define and appreciate your child's *imprint.*

For at least two parents, this exercise did exactly that.

The first of our two scenarios involves Todd, a parent to a 13-year-old teenage son, Erik. No doubt about it, Todd is one *proud* parent who regards Erik as one multi-talented young man. He seems to perform well whether it is on the soccer field, the field of math, or the theatrical stage. Yet, to condense the life patterns of Erik in order to better describe his *imprint*, well, Dad has never done that.

Nor has Debra. She is a single mother of three children, including Johnny, a 10-year-old third grader. Johnny is the product of a troubled home situation with limited opportunities. This fact, coupled by a learning disability, resulted in Johnny being held back a year following second grade. Despite this, Debra sees sparks of brilliance in Johnny that gives her a genuine sense of optimism.

Both Todd and Debra completed the 15 item *Imprint* questionnaire and identified the following:

Question	Erik	Johnny
1. What comes naturally & when do they shine?	Sports Math Problem solving Being on stage Responding to pressure Playing soccer Rock climbing	Various computer games Carefully drawing a picture Measuring things accurately
2. What do they enjoy in their? leisure or playtime?	Roller blading Going to camp Winning Being with friends Playing all sports	Riding his bike Playing computer games Recess Drawing a picture
3. What work experiences have they enjoyed?	Snow blowing Door-to-door sales (enjoyed earning $$!)	(Too young to work)
4. Whom have they admired and why?	Dad (values) Sunday School teacher (fun)	(no one mentioned)
5. What do they talk about?	E. Sports	B. The latest computer game
6. What do they like to read?	E. *Sports Illustrated*	(could not think of anything)
7. What would they like to receive free tutoring in?	B. Math A. Theater	B. Computers

8. "What I Did in my Summer Vacation?"	E. Backpacking trip	F. The weekend at Grandma's
9. What did your child receive praise for?	F. Working well with others	C. Art skills
10. What subjects does your child enjoy most?	E. Physical Education	C. Art
11. How would they describe their favorite teacher?	D. He allows us to move about	C. She uses lots of pictures and designs
12. What type of teacher does your child prefer?	E. A sports fanatic F. A teacher who talks about celebrities	B. A cool, logical teacher C. A teacher who is into art
13. What annoys your child?	G. Failure to achieve good grades	B. Disruptions, such as a computer breakdown
14. What sounds most like your child?	F. Organizing an activity or game	C. Assembling a new piece of electronic equipment
15. What department or college at EU are they apt to enroll in?	F. Communications or Business	C. College of Arts & Design

After reviewing this information about Erik and Johnny, you've probably surmised some things about both young men. So did their parents. Todd sees his son as one who thrives on challenges and the rewards associated with accomplishing those goals. He also sees him as a socialite, but is delighted to observe him as comfortable in approaching persons of any age or background. Despite Erik's "take charge" attitude, there's also a softer part of him that reaches out to others.

What Johnny might lack in Erik's assertive disposition is a more private personality that often plays out in a combination of things artistic, precise, and imaginative. Give Johnny a chance to play on the school's Apple computer, and you have one happy camper. If only he had such a tool at home. Fortunately, his teacher recognizes the same and is doing her utmost in locating a used one for him and his family.

So, on the one hand we have a take-charge, problem solver (Erik). On the other, an imaginative designer (Johnny). The *imprint* process is beginning to take form. Yet, let's be honest, a few more dots need to be connected. Todd and Debra are able to attach those courtesy of the next chapter. And, so will you.

Yet, before doing that, some other important ingredients are necessary to develop a more complete, meaningful, and useful *imprint?* Try on these four suggestions:

1. "Group-Think"

If you believe that nobody knows your own kid quite like you, think again. Let's be honest. As parents, we're usually guilty of wearing rose-colored glasses in assessing those many, many attributes of our flesh-and-blood. But there are others in the lives of our kids who seem them in action and in ways that offer a small or totally different perspective. I'll never forget my parents getting insights from my fraternity brothers about me that left them saying, "Are we talking about the same Mark de Roo?"

Those other persons in our children's lives—friends, teachers, coaches, youth group leaders, grandparents, and fraternity brothers—also have insights about your kids that only make the picture more complete and really representative. But those insights only remain the occasional compliment or comment, unless, as parents, you become a bit of a Sherlock Holmes and are game to inquire about how they see your daughter's skills, orientation, personality, and values.

There's a fair chance, you'll hear some things that might shock you. You might hear a variety of perceptions, ranging from "She's a real leader!" to "He's able to troubleshoot a hardware problem in no time flat" to "Her ability to improvise is unbelievable!" These are things 180 degrees different from what you ever expected to hear. Then again, they might not be any surprise at all. Yet, as my father often said, "You won't know, unless you ask." So, ask. Talk to their friends. Chat with your child's teacher at Parent-Teacher conferences. Listen carefully. And, of course, write them down, adding to your own list as you go.

2. Patterns

Our daughter, Hillary, has a Sunday morning tradition like most Americans: she loves the Sunday paper. Woven into the Comics section is *Magic Eye: the 3D Illusion Puzzle.* These are the puzzles that have a conglomeration of colors and indistinguishable shapes that somehow disguise a three-dimensional image. Perhaps, you've done them. I've tried and have been successful a few times. Then there's Hillary—the master illusion problem solver. Without exception, she'll solve every one of those puzzles in seconds. She doesn't even have to press it upon her nose and gradually move it away as the instructions suggest. Intuitively, she knows the secret. She cleverly allows her mind to make sense of *all* the overlying patterns while not focusing on just one dimension. It's literally looking at the forest for the trees.

The same principle applies in identifying the *imprint* of your children. The overlaying patterns for them will require an analysis of their life stages from pre-school through high school. As you think about your daughter or son's development, what patterns can you observe? What traits, for instance, have been rather consistent? Which ones seem to gain obvious strength with time? What typically has been a "turn-on" for them? What does this say about what they value?

As you do so, it's important *not* to exploit one event, a one-time remark from a teacher, or singular achievement.. What you want to focus on is their overall *modus operandi*—their MO—how they typically act and play, how they usually express themselves, and what it is they typically love to do. It's helpful to take a moment to comment or write down those consistent or emerging traits, values, and skills that have been particular to each of their life or school stages—and then, checking for those similarities between each stage. See a pattern? I bet you do. Identify them, affirm them, and then, build upon them—which we'll shortly address in the next chapter.

And by the way, if your child is simply too young to draw any perceptions for the moment, here's a suggestion. Maintain annual lists. A good time to do this is either on their birthday or around Thanksgiving, a particularly appropriate time to reflect on each member of your family.

3. Daydream

When was the last time you daydreamed? I did it a lot in school. I think my teachers thought I was an alien because I often was startled by the exclamation, "Earth to Mark!" It was a lot of fun then. It still is. It gives me or anyone an opportunity to think about what might be. It's hopeful speculation. Well, for the moment, you have been granted "Official Authorization to Daydream" on behalf of your child.

Your task is to daydream, speculate, envision, whatever on how you might be able to cultivate some of the patterns you're discerning about your child. For example, if you're sensing an "artistic" flair within your child, how might you be able to develop this talent? Here are a few possibilities:

- Enroll your daughter or son in a leisure-time class in Community Education program or at a local Arts Council
- Talk to your child's teacher or art instructor for their suggestions on things to do

- Have him/her participate in a special project, such a designing a poster or constructing a model
- Visit an art gallery.

Your child will either get pumped about these things or balk big-time. Then again, they may be somewhere in between. If they're ambivalent, test the waters. Try at least two activities and check their response. Whether you leave such activities at a couple or a couple dozen, all of these experiences will verify a level of interest and aptitude. If the aptitude is innate, the interest will follow. And probably with such spirit and enthusiasm that you'll feel blown away. But what could be better!

4. P.A.E.

Several years ago, I added one brief exercise to my daily devotions. I started reading an old, threadbare copy of a church hymnal that our choir director decided to put out to pasture. Yes, *reading* it, not singing it. By unanimous consent within my family, the latter was simply not an option. OK, I can live with that, even if it is *their* loss. At any rate, I soon found myself really hearing the words despite the fact that I had sung some of those hymns more times than I could count. It's proven to be something special.

One hymn, which really stood out in a new way, was #385: *What a Friend We Have in Jesus*. Check out the lines of the first stanza:

O what peace we often forfeit, O what needless pain we bear,
All because we do not carry everything to God in prayer!

It's really a pretty simple message: Pray About Everything. Or, P.A.E. You see, we don't have to go it alone. And as the verse indicates, we can take <u>everything</u> to God in prayer. That includes your concerns. Your career. Your elderly next door neighbor. The Middle East. Saturday's picnic. Your kids. The friends they choose. Their teachers. Your child's career.

And this process. By partnering with the good Lord, I truly believe that road map will become a whole lot more meaningful.

So, a quick summary of this chapter. We've highlighted the importance of such things as gifts, imprints, personality, divine guidance, and a few other choice items. All are components of a process for determining our vocational lot in life. No one can do this process for your child better than you. As a parent, you've inherited that opportunity. Thankfully, no special certifications or degrees are required. It's simply a privilege that comes with the territory.

Since your child is a constant work-in-progress, this process also needs on-going attention and assistance. The questions and qualifiers in this chapter are something you'll want to revisit occasionally. You'll be prompted to do this as you encourage your child to uncover aspects about themselves through interacting with the sights, sounds, textures, challenges, and wonders of our contemporary world and God's creation.

But, now—at long last—it's time to bring all this together. Now that you have a better understanding of what makes and moves your child, you're itching to ask the question: what career options make sense for my child? After all, it's probably one of the reasons you acquired this book. Well, to uncover them, just turn the page and let the drum roll begin!

Chapter V

Making Connections—Career Connections

It's Christmastime, and your Aunt Emily thinks you need something mindless to do in your "spare time." So, she presents you a gift: needlepoint. It's the same sort of gift that Rosey Grier, the ex-National Football League lineman, confessed to doing as part of his "softer side." Actually, she gives you something that is a close cousin: a counted cross-stitch sampler kit. It's not exactly your style, but somehow you manage the customary, "Oh, you shouldn't have" and then proceed to open the package and examine its contents.

First, you discover that "floss" is different than what you use in your teeth; it's the thread. Next, you come upon the actual fabric that lacks the paint-by-number pattern, which would make things a whole lot easier. They're serious—you actually have to count the stitches to create the design. And finally, you come upon one other item: the instructions. You begin to shudder if it reads in any way like a Math textbook. Here what it says:

Please read this entire set of instructions before weaving the sampler:

1. *Each length of embroidery floss consists of 6 threads—or strands—twisted together. Cut your floss the length you need and pull one strand of floss at a time.*

2. *Begin stitching in the middle of your sampler so that the design is centered on the linen.*

(Let's skip a few. They're just about making knots anyway.)

3. *Be sure to include your own initials and the current year in an inconspicuous place. When your sampler is framed, please complete the an information label with your name, town, and date and attach it to the paper on the back of your frame.*

You respectfully stuff the floss, fabric, and instructions back in the package. You think that a tie would be the lesser of two evils and certainly a lot less work. Maybe, you'll find some spare time to do the sampler—like in your retirement.

Well, if, per chance, you've ever attempted any sort of stitching, weaving, crocheting, etc., the above set of instructions probably appears quite familiar. However, when I'm about to spend a zillion hours in eyestrain, poked fingers, and lost needles (I'm speaking from experience), these introductory words strike me as anything but, well, inspirational. After all, shouldn't a set of instructions, whether it's for a VCR or your child's bike, begin with a little RAH-RAH, something to get the juices flowing?

I think professional needle pointers, or at least those that compose instructions, should learn a lesson or two from those marketing types that creatively fashion and assemble the *J. Peterman Clothes* catalog. If you know anything about this catalog, each article of clothing is set in the imaginary context of something adventuresome, romantic, or historic. Maybe, this would be their alternative to the above:

> *From generation to generation, these simple yet carefully detailed samplers told a story—or a pearl of wisdom. Somehow, those that wove thread-upon-thread must have known that a keepsake was in the making. If they did not, they certainly would not have carefully*

> *selected the azure blue, the soft pink, or the striking gold that made each piece of burlap an artist's canvas. As you begin weaving this mid-18th century design, transform yourself to a back porch in colonial Virginia where each completed stoke of the needle was followed by conversation with other weavers. There was talk of forcing King George to repeal a tea tax. Maybe, it would even come to revolution. With the future uncertain, who knows what might happen to this sampler? Still, you continue stitching. Only now, it has heightened significance.*

OK, it's more than a *little* melodramatic. Hey, we're talking about nothing more than making a counted cross-stitch, for heaven's sake. I guess that's true—to a degree. Yet, too often, we diminish an activity before we even have a moment to appreciate it. Maybe, we should give both the final product as well as the process of getting there a bit more regard. In some cases, even some reverence.

I particularly think this is so when one projects an activity into something bigger than life. Like planning one's life. Or one's career. And I can't think of a more appropriate metaphor for doing so than the process of cross-stitching or weaving.

It begins with separating the strands and appreciating each one for its distinctive color. In the scenario of designing a career path, it is a recognition of the fibers of our lives. In each of us are the strands of personality, values, skill orientation, and an array of others. Left in isolation, they have value, yet limited. Weaving offers a challenge for those fibers to become integrated. It's interlacing those strands of who we are. And if it's executed carefully, they coalesce into a coherent whole. Yes, the whole—the career planning whole—is certainly more than just the sum of its parts.

So, it's time to weave. Well, almost. You'll be asked in a moment to identify a few more strands that will aid in creating a profile on your child and suggesting some specific career possibilities. To begin, however, you'll need you to pull up the results from that Chapter IV where you were asked to answer several questions. All your answers to those questions will be helpful, but your responses to items, 5-15 will be especially instructive. Take a few moments to review your answers.

Then, for questions 5-15, you'll want to add up the number of checks for each question by letter. In other words, add up the number of checks for all the "A" statements, the checks for all the "B," and continuing until you complete tallying all the checks for the remaining statements. Multiply that number of checks for each letter by 10. As an example, if you had 3 checks for the "E" statements, your Preference Score for that area will be "30."

OK, so where are we going with this? Well, the answers to questions 5-15 and the careers that build upon those answers are all based upon the research of Dr. Howard Gardner, the Harvard University educator, researcher, and respected pioneer of the concept of "multiple intelligences."

That's intelligences with an "s." Dr. Gardner uses this term to characterize a person's natural talents, <u>not</u> necessarily a measure of one's cerebral or mental capacity. Each of us has them. They simply vary by intensity among different areas. Here's a brief explanation of each intelligence:

- **Verbal/Linguistic Intelligence**—the ability to read, write, and communicate with words. Authors, journalists, poets, orators, and comedians are examples of people with verbal intelligence. Today, more than ever, virtually all career fields require strong communication skills.
- **Technological/Mathematical Intelligence**—the ability to reason and calculate—to think things through in a logical, systematic manner. These are the kinds of skills highly developed in engineers, scientists, economists, accountants, detectives, and members of the legal profession.
- **Visual Intelligence**—the ability to think in pictures, visualize a future result—to imagine things in your mind's eye. You use this

skill when you have a sense of direction or when you have to navigate or draw. Architects, artists, sculptors, sailors, photographers, and strategic planners have this talent.

- **Auditory/Musical Intelligence**—the ability to learn and apply a second language or to sense changes in volume, pitch, or rhythm. It's a talent obviously enjoyed by musicians, composers, recording engineers, translators, and speech pathologists.
- **Kinesthetic/Motor Intelligence**—the ability to use your body skillfully to solve problems, create products or present ideas and emotions. This is a talent obviously used for athletic pursuits, artistic pursuits such as dancing or acting, or in building and construction. People, ranging from surgeons to toolmakers that are "good with their hands," fall into this category.
- **Interpersonal Intelligence**—the ability to work effectively with others, to relate to other people and display empathy and understanding—and to notice motivations and goals. This is a vital talent exhibited by good teachers, facilitators, therapists, politicians, and sales people.
- **Intrapersonal Intelligence**—the ability for self-analysis and reflection—to be able to quietly contemplate and assess one's accomplishments, review behavior and innermost feelings, to make plans and set goals—to know oneself. Philosophers, counselors, and many peak performers in all fields of endeavor have this talent.
- **Naturalist/Scientific Intelligence**—the ability to recognize flora and fauna, to make other consequential distinctions in the natural world and to use this talent productively in, for example, fishing, farming, or biological science. Farmers, botanists, conservationists, biologists, and environmentalists would all this display this skill.
- **Philosophical/Religious**—having the passion and skills to create a more just society and to work toward a better world either locally or globally.

With these descriptions, you are probably confirming your own intelligence and speculating on your child's. I know I did. For instance, Ingrid, our daughter, has a high ability in "interpersonal" intelligence with secondary intelligences in both "intrapersonal" and "philosophical/religious." Her intelligence in the "logical/mathematical" is a whole other matter. Once you've done that, you are ready to get into the really fun part: putting it together and discovering options. Begin by ranking your child's intelligences based on their scores. The intelligence area with the highest score will be their dominant intelligence. The next lowest scores will be your child's "complementary" intelligence. Please note the next two highest scores as complementary intelligences. For instance, you might have a son with a "Naturalist/Scientific" intelligence score of 40 with a complementary score of 30 in the "Technological/Math" area and an "Interpersonal" score of 20.

Next, the good stuff. You'll find a complete list of careers that are consistent with you child's ranked sequence of intelligences in Appendix F. What you'll find there are suggested careers that match your child's preferred sequence of intelligences. Here's an example: a social worker has a profile of "I/V/S." This suggests that a social worker should be dominant in the "interpersonal" intelligence (I) area followed by complementary intelligences in "verbal/linguistic" (V) and "intrapersonal" (S).

In reviewing the list that matches your child's ranked sequence, keep in mind a couple of things. First, the list careers in the Appendix are only a few among the many. A host of other careers exists in the world of work. Secondly, these are only suggested options and not a firm prescription. They are only meant to spur some thinking and perhaps, some further investigation and interest. Thirdly, while some careers might surprise you, other ones will not. And that's good! It's a confirmation of your thinking.

A quick note about this last point. Seeing various career options for your child conjures up all sorts of images, ranging from sports psychologist to cyber librarian. Some of those options may excite you to the point of wanting to schedule your daughter for a job interview next Monday.

Other ones may truly bore you. Others you may know much or very little about. Therefore, a word of caution. Watch out for your perceptions, your images from times past, and your stereotypes. Many of those careers may be different than what you think or once thought. I mean, *very* different. With the substance of careers seemingly changing by the minute, many occupations have undergone major transformations. Think about your own career and the changes your vocation has experienced.

Keeping your own stereotypes in check while exploring the particular details of an occupation for your son or daughter requires a check of a different sort: a "reality" check. Learning about various options is fundamental. It's also the departure point for the next phase of the career planning process. Not fully exploring both the basics and the nuances of an occupation is playing with fire. How many times have you encountered someone who studied and prepared for a certain career only to find out that the job was 180 degrees different than what was touted?

Fortunately, there are innumerable ways of learning about careers, but they fall into two primary categories. The first method is reading. Tons of excellent descriptions about general career fields and specific job are available in the library, a school's counseling office, your local bookstore, or on the web. Snapshots of various careers can be found in *The Dictionary of Occupational Titles* to the full-length, unabridged descriptions of specific occupations as can be found, for example, in *Careers for English Majors.* Always check out the copyright date on each resource. Libraries often resemble attics and contain relics from way back in time. The scope, qualifications, and use of technology in different jobs are changing every day. For instance, most career-related books make little reference to the use or application of computers within an occupation.

Other books or guides worth reading are:

- Occupational Outlook Handbook (US. Dept. of Labor)
- Occupational Outlook Quarterly (US Dept. of Labor; quarterly periodical)

- Guide to Occupational Exploration
- Encyclopedia of Careers & Vocational Guidance by Dr. William Hopke
- 100 Jobs in Technology by Lori Hawkins and Betsey Dowling
- Jobs Almanac (Adams Media Corp.)
- Job Smarts 50 Top Careers by Bradley Richardson
- 101 Careers — A+ Guide to the Fastest Growing Opportunities by John Harkavy

The second method is talking—talking with people who perform their jobs day in and day out. By talking with working people, your son or daughter will get to know the job "up close and personal." Not only will they gather some valuable information, but they get to *feel* the job through the experience of someone else. They'll sense the job by how pumped the person is when describing their job. Or, how much they're not. Children are particularly adept at reading people.

In this regard, it's helpful to talk to more than one person about the same job. You'll never know when that first person's bad experience with their career may be the next ten persons' unbelievably fantastic experience. Or, vice versa. I know this all-too-well following an experience I had mid-way through my junior year in college.

Until that time in college, I was a pre-law major. During our Christmas break, I had lunch with a family friend who happened to be an attorney. I wanted to pick his brain about his experience in the law. For a solid hour, I heard nothing but a litany of criticisms, disheartening experiences with clients, and personal regrets. Imagine how I felt at the end of that lunch! I left there wondering what, in earth, I had done with nearly three years of college. Shortly thereafter, I made a decision to change majors.

While I don't regret the decision to switch majors, I often wonder if I had been premature in my decision. What if I talked to a few other attorneys whose experience was just the opposite?

Talking with many persons about their careers is part of the larger process of "information interviewing," a term coined by *the* icon in career planning, Richard Bolles (author of *What Color is Your Parachute?*). Information interviewing goes beyond the basics of a penned job description. The process reveals the special nuances of an occupation, the formulas for success or failure, and the personalities of those who make their particular job their livelihood and part of their identity. A few of tips for conducting an information interview include:

1. Identifying persons who genuinely enjoy their jobs.
2. Asking some key questions. See Appendix E for a list of questions. Here's a sample:
   A. What are your responsibilities?
   B. What parts of the job do you like more? Less?
   C. What type of training or education is necessary?
   D. Who or what caused you to get into this type of job?
   E. Is this a career with lots of potential?
   F. How do you use technology in your job?
   G. What makes some persons in this job really successful and other ones less so?
3. Interviewing someone on their home turf, i.e., their work place.
4. Sending the person a "thank you" note following the information interview.

Occasionally, it's tough to identify whom your son or daughter can interview if the option is one you've rarely or never heard about. Chances are, however, that your network of friends and co-workers will locate the name of someone who is performing that occupation. Or, try your local Chamber of Commerce. Better yet, use the Internet. Chat rooms can supply lots of valuable information. On a practical note, one never knows when that information interview will lead to something bigger and better. Years later that same person might be the first person to contact when networking not *about* a job, but *for* a job.

Gathering the information through articles, the Internet, or networking may sound like "research." It is. But, it doesn't take a degree in scientific research or investigative reporting.

Nor is it defined as an adult activity. If anything, checking out career options should be a shared process. Having your daughter or son assume some of the responsibility for learning about each option is important. It's certainly developmental. It has them learning to ask questions—with courtesy. It requires them to be assertive and inquisitive. And hopefully, it breaks down stereotypes.

Summary

Intelligences. Skill groups. Creating connections and identifying options. Information interviewing. All are components of shaping one's vocational direction. Think about the majority of individuals, however, who has never thought about, let alone mixed, those components for the sake of their career. Who would wish that for anyone? In particular, who would wish that upon their children?

One more thing. This process is not a one-time event. In fact, it's one of those things you'll hopefully do often for and with your children. It's part of growing up. And as your child learns more about themselves, new options will present themselves. The key phrase is "learning more about themselves." And as you do that, new dots will be connected. Such a process for your kids requires little more than a loving facilitator, prompter, and encourager. Thankfully, you're that very person. Way to go!

Chapter VI

Special Needs for Special Folks

Some people are saints. Perhaps, they don't have the notoriety of Joan of Arc, Francis of Assisi, or even jolly old St. Nick, but they certainly meet the qualifications. Well, several years ago, I had the good fortune of not only knowing one, but also working for one. His name was Eric Heiberg.

I first met Eric when I interviewed for a human resources position at Herman Miller, Inc., the office furniture people. Eric held the position of Corporate Staffing Manager. Fearing the worst—you know, the drill-sergeant type—I was primed and prepared. Within a few seconds, however, I shed my defenses. This guy didn't have a military flattop. In fact, he didn't have much hair at all. What I encountered was a person with a special blend of ease and informality. No calling him "Mr. Heiberg." It was "Eric." And he had a smile that wouldn't stop. You couldn't help but like the guy!

Thankfully, I landed the job at Herman Miller and thus began a long-standing professional and personal relationship with Eric. While I worked for him, I admired his creativity at sourcing potential hires. I studied his knack for discerning a prospect's true tendencies when conducting interviews. I loved his fan-like elation when a candidate accepted a job offer—he'd shoot his arms skyward like he just scored a touchdown. Most importantly, I marveled at his ability to maintain an upbeat attitude and a smile on his face despite the pressures of recruiting strong talent for a Fortune 500 company.

Oh, by the way, did I mention that Eric suffers from muscular dystrophy?

For years, Eric has been battling this progressive disease. When I first knew him, it was apparent in his slight leaning to one side. The lack of muscle tone created difficulty in standing totally erect. In the years that I've known him, the disease has twisted and reduced his stature by nearly a foot. Now, he's confined to an Amigo and a modified van. The disease has advanced to the point that it has become sufficiently debilitating, leading to an early retirement. Despite his condition, Eric serves his community on a local city commission and he wouldn't miss a local college basketball game come rain, snow, or dead of night. More importantly, the man continues to generate an optimistic and cheery spirit. A quintessential gentleman if I ever met one.

When first mentioning Eric's disability, what happened to your perception? Besides being surprised, did you feel some sympathy or somehow different? Most of us extend such feelings, however small, to discounting a physically disabled person's skills and abilities. We do so as a result of a series of life-long messages, some direct and others more subtle.

And, our perceptions are not limited to the physically disabled. Virtually anyone deemed a member of a "protected" class senses it. A Native American knows it. So does an Asian American. Those folks over age 40 have felt it. Certainly, those individuals labeled "learning disabled" know the experience. And, ironically, so do those persons on the other end of the spectrum: the gifted and talented.

This chapter is about them. More significantly, it's *for* them. Yet, it's really for every one of us. We'll approach the subject with a twofold purpose. One is to dispel some myths and some of our perceptions. A second purpose will be to offer a few career planning tools for those young people fitting a "category" and for those of us who want to care. Our focus will include the disabled, gifted-and-talented, urban persons of color, and lastly, young women. My only regret in this chapter, due to space constraints, is not discussing other groups and individuals.

Students with Disabilities

During a time when much attention has been given to the topic of "diversity," here's a trivia question. Which is the largest minority group in our schools yet is generally given the lowest priority? The answer may surprise you: persons with disabilities. The absence of minimal attention granted this group reveals some likely consequences:

- 29% of persons with disabilities are employed
- Of those disabled adults that work, 30% have annual incomes of less than $15,000
- 20% of persons with disabilities fail to finish high school, compared to 10% of non-disabled persons (Lou Harris poll—1998)

Yet, things are not entirely all gloom-and-doom. The Americans with Disabilities Act (ADA) seems to have been the spark to change the mind-set of employers and the hopes of those persons with disabilities. Since the passage of the ADA in 1991, some new trends are emerging:

- By 2000, the number of disabled Americans employed rose to 49.7 million or 19% of the U.S. population (U.S. Census Bureau).
- College enrollments for people with disabilities leapt from 29% to 44%.
- In 1997, 56% of Americans shopped during the holiday season at retailers associated with a cause, such as companies actively employing persons with disabilities.
- Employers are recognizing that the cost of accommodating workers with disabilities is not nearly as expensive as originally feared. Most accommodations cost an average of $45 and almost 75% cost nothing.
- Technological advances are eliminating many of the physical and informational barriers that are common to persons with disabilities.

Two of the above trends require some additional comment. Our shift to an information-based economy lends itself nicely to persons with disability.

Internet and World Wide Web access requires skills of the "knowledge worker" and little, if any, physical demands typically associated with workers in a manufacturing setting. Microsoft Corporation provides an "accessibility wizard" in its Windows '98 software that enables users to find all the accessibility options of their products. The World Wide Web Consortium has initiated a program to provide Web functionality for persons with disabilities.

The advances in technology have also offered dramatic new career and learning opportunities for persons with specific disabilities. The unbelievable advances in computer technology, in particular, are giving a new meaning to "accessibility" that would have seemed impossible less than a generation ago. Here are some examples:

- Paralyzed from the neck down in a motorcycle accident, Mark Harmon is a specialist at Unum Corp., an insurance conglomerate. He offers advice to people with disabilities via e-mail, faxes, the phone, and the web. His tool? A software program called *DragonDictate.* It is a voice-activated program that allows him to control his PC while navigating among his applications. (*Computerworld,* Sept., 1998)
- Kids with cerebral palsy or Down's syndrome can use a compact 8" x 7", touch-screen communicator, permitting people to select words, letters, or phrases. They touch the particular image or icon on the screen and a voice speaks and up to 30 words per minute. (*Business Week,* May 25, 1998)
- Voice technology has aided the blind in significant ways. IBM Japan Ltd. uses a computer-synthesized voice male voice to read normal text; it switches to a female voice when it encounters hyperlinks to other Web sites.
- In the near future, it is likely that a computer-screen cursor will be able to follow the path of a person's eyes for those disabled persons unable to use a mouse.

While technology, the ADA, plus increased federal and state funds for the disabled are helping, a more significant hurdle remains: a change in attitude. And a change in temperament requires more than legislation and dollars. This is germane to individuals with any type of disability, including physical, mental impairment, learning disability, emotional impairment, speech and language impairments, etc.

What is necessary is a mindset by teachers, employers, and other support personnel, which comes to view people with disabilities as having genuine potential. This is particularly necessary for parents. All of us respond to an implied or stated level of expectation. Great expectations yield higher results. Low expectations, low results. If such a foundation is forsaken, a person's self-esteem is diminished and their career prospects are jeopardized or, at worst, condemned to failure.

When this premise is affirmed, then the person's particular characteristics can be addressed. Several key strategies need to be developed in connection with the special requirements of the individual. This brief chapter cannot begin to model or elaborate the specific strategies for the variety of young persons that have varying types and degrees of a disability. Each type of disability warrants its own evaluation. Thankfully, there are a multitude of resources and specialists with voluminous information. And, they are just a phone call away, starting with the Yellow Pages (Human Services) or on the Internet.

For a young person with a disability, the focus must be within the school setting. When planning a school curriculum or a career, a collection of common factors should be considered in the context of the disability. While some of them may have no consequence, others might. If so, a young person's disability may have an impact on the following factors—an impact that may determine how a person approaches life-long learning and living:

- Attention
- Oral language

- Perception
- Problem solving
- Reading
- Motor tasks
- Making judgments
- Social interaction
- Emotional development
- Acquisition of learning strategies
- Vocational and career education

Following an evaluation of a young person's disability in the context of these factors, a specially designed program is necessary. *Critically* necessary. Many parents, teachers, and resource personnel either separately or collectively create an *Individual Development Plan* (IDP) or an *Individual Educational Program* (IEP) that speaks to the unique learning characteristics and requirements of each student or person. Cookie-cutter approaches just don't make it. In some states, IDPs/IEPs are required by law and require annual assessments with input from a team of parents, teachers, tutors, and resource professionals. While IDPs/IEPs incorporate specific elements that are particular to each person, they don't isolate the individual. In fact, students with disabilities should remain in the general educational environment unless the disability is of such a severe nature that a regular educational program is simply unsatisfactory. The significance of individualized assessments avoids the more common practice of tracking persons by categories, not their capabilities.

While the initiation of an IDP/IEP might begin with mom & dad, the orchestration of all these factors need not be a solo effort, particularly when charting some career options. In the case of young persons with disabilities, it indeed takes "a whole village to raise one child." In some villages, cities, and towns, successful models have been designed and implemented. One such model is the Student Driven Collaborative

Transitioning model in Kenosha, Wisconsin. The components of their program include:

- A clearly defined program mission statement
- High quality leadership and staff
- Access to extensive and updated published research
- Academic and vocational education
- Vocational assessment
- Career training and/or on-the-job training
- Effective collaborative relationships between the schools, businesses, community service agencies, local colleges, and, of course, the parents
- A focus on the individual's particular needs

In summary, more and more resources are being rallied for persons with disabilities. Those resources—community, technology, governmental—are creating some of the small revolutions that are occurring daily for the 54 million Americans that possess some type of disability. Such revolutions are providing meaningful and varied career opportunities for the Eric Heibergs, the Mark Harmons, and other disabled individuals. Equally, if not of greater importance, they offer hope for persons too often shunned, misunderstood, and ignored. That hope is long overdue. For more information on resources for disabled individuals, check out these web sites:

- National Organization for Disability <www.nod.org>
- AbleNet Foundation <www.ablenet.org>
- National Alliance of the Disabled <www.naotd.org>
- Worldwide Virtual Community of the Disabled <www.linkable.org>
- President's Committee on the Employment of People with Disabilities <www.50.pcedpd.gov/pcepd/>

Gifted Young People

The dateline is the fall of '72. I'm student teaching at Holland Christian High School. This semester is a real biggie for me as a prospective teacher. Either I do the job or my entire educational program and four years of big-time tuition payments are down the tubes. I've been assigned to teach two classes: American History and American Government.

Between the two, the Government class poses the largest challenge. But, it isn't due to the material. The spectrum of intelligence and personalities make for a convoluted bell curve. It is anchored on the one side by Kurt, the classic goof-off, party animal, and resident jokester. The other side is the singular domain of Jack. What Jack lacks in EQ (emotional quotient), he more than compensates with his IQ. It becomes immediately apparent that Jack will push me. He'd causes me to create taxing lessons plans, requiring three times as much material and ten times the amount of prep time.

Enter James Joubert, my supervising teacher. As most supervising teachers go, Mr. Joubert probably deserves no more than a C-. He's light on observation and heavy on interaction, at least with his peers in the teachers' lounge where the smoke rivals any downtown bar. Occasionally, he extracts himself from the haze with a provocative question for me, "Well, Mr. de Roo, how's it goin'?" I once thought it would be cool to tell him, "Well, we role-played the Boston Tea Party by throwing all the desks and chairs out the window!" Yeah, I only thought about it. Reality and the need for an "A" suggested otherwise.

Anyway, I had a serious question for him about Jack. "Mr. Joubert, I'm stumped about what to do with Jack. Jack knows the material as well as me. Maybe better. How do I stimulate him in class while teaching the other twenty-five students?" I hoped that twenty plus years of teaching affords anyone some measure of wisdom. Even Mr. Joubert. "First," he says, "meet with him privately and check out his interest in the topic. If he indicates an interest in learning about, let's say, the criminal justice system, think about giving him a special project that can continue that interest. Secondly, he knows he's operating at a different level than his classmates, and he most likely understands your dilemma. So, include him when you can and do a couple of extra things for him." Those occasional snippets of insight from Mr. Joubert are the road signs that kept me going. OK, let's give him a B+ instead of that C-.

The story doesn't end there. During the remainder of the semester, I learned that I wasn't alone. Jack's other teachers in physics, English literature, and trigonometry were confronted with the same challenge. Seems that Jack was just plain good at most everything. And Jack's situation is often typical of many other gifted and talented individuals. It's what psychologists have come to regard as *multipotentiality* or the potential to develop any number of options due to a wide variety of interests, numerous aptitudes, and typically strong abilities.

While having a multiplicity of abilities can be viewed as a blessing, it also poses some particular career challenges. Specifically, how does one decide among the smorgasbord of interests and vocational options? Jim Delisle and Judy Galbraith in their book, *The Gifted Kids Survival Guide II,* share a few experiences of such folk:

> *"I ended up teaching at a university, but not until I'd toyed with the fields of psychiatry, pediatrics, and forestry."*
>
> Jim, 33

> *"I got my B.A. in psychology, worked for an orchestra, went to business school for my M.B.A., and now I'm a vice president of a software company. I may have arrived by an indirect route, but I like where I am."*
>
> Leah, 36

> *"I work in advertising, I enjoy it, and I'm good at it, but I also take flying lessons on the weekends and I wonder—is it too late to apply to astronaut school?"*
>
> Tania, 30

Due to their diversity and extraordinary levels of ability, it's easy to assume that the gifted and talented are equally adept at decision-making and that career planning will take care of itself. Wrong assumption. Evidence is mounting that youthful brilliance in one or more areas does not translate into adult satisfaction and accomplishment in working life. When a young person displays a wide variety of interests and abilities, it often increases the complexity of decision-making and frequently delays it.

Recent developments in counseling models are helping to recognize some signs of multiplicity and some solutions. Here are a few at different stages of schooling:

Elementary:

Indicators:

Sporadic periods of enthusiasm

Difficulty in finishing up and following

Intervention Strategies:

Encourage focusing activities, such as Scout merit badges that require follow through

Provide realistic exposure to world of work through trips to parents' work places

Middle School:

Indicators:

Participate in numerous social and recreational activities

Over-schedule course load

Intervention Strategies:

Encourage them to prioritize and select only a few extracurricular activities

Provide for light volunteer work
Provide "shadowing" experiences

Senior High:

Indicators:

Packed class schedules

Leadership roles in a myriad of school groups, religious activities, and community organizations

Vocational test results that show interests in a large number of occupations

Intervention Strategies:

Provide value-based guidance that fulfills deeply held values

Discourage conformist, stereotyped job choices

Encourage visits to colleges in a few areas of interest

Offer more extensive volunteer work or paid internships with professionals

College Students:

Indicators:

Multiple academic majors

Frequent switching of college majors

Intense participation in extracurricular activities

May make hasty or arbitrary career choices

Intervention Strategies:

Seek career counseling based on an assessment of values, interests, and needs

Avoid conformist major choices

Seek a mentor
Encourage significant internship or off-campus opportunities
Focus on long-term goal setting and planning

While society marvels at the Thomas Jeffersons and Ben Franklins who had multiple talents, there are the Bill Gates of our era who have more of a singular focus. The founder of *Microsoft* demonstrated an early but singular affinity for computers. His mother and some like-minded moms who raised money to purchase the room-sized version of an early computer for their school fostered this interest in large part. Bill and his pioneering colleagues are examples of persons with *early emergence.* Such children have one or two areas of unusually high intellect. As a consequence, they usually possess a rather tight career focus. One or two careers have interest for them for a long time. Sometimes, for a lifetime.

If you're a parent of an early emergent child, there's an easy invitation to neglect or diminish a super-strong interest of a child in favor of a well-rounded approach. After all, there's so much more to life than just *one* thing, right? On the other hand, some parents perceive an early talent in their child and hastily respond with over-indulgence in the form of all the latest-and-greatest gadgets, software, books, technology, etc. In either case, it's often the child that suffers and whose special interest may be shattered. Parents of early emerging kids are encouraged to affirm their child for their special talent as well as providing some additional resources and even some training.

Unlike myself, I have a friend who loves technology, especially all the current audio/visual stuff. His family room looks more like a showroom straight from SONY or Technics. Well, it didn't take long for his youngest son, Scott, to fall in love with all the buttons and dials this equipment had to offer. It took even less time for Scott to imagine himself as "The Youngest DJ on Christian Radio." Which is exactly what he became at age

11. Every Sunday afternoon, Scott could be heard on western Michigan's dominant Christian radio station. Between Sundays, Scott was and is dubbing things, experimenting with the technology to create a fascinating sound or a new format. His dad provides some occasional expertise, but after a while it's difficult to know who is the teacher and who is the student. Scott's talent rivals persons five times his age.

So, what are some signs—and suggestions—for other Scotts or persons with signs or *early emergence?*

Elementary School:

Indicators:

Avid interest in one school subject

Writes more papers on one area of interest than in other subjects

Only fair performance in other areas outside of primary interest

Intervention strategies:

Encourage fantasies through reading biographies

Provide opportunities to socialize with kids of similar interests

Consult with experts on the nature of gifts and talents

Middle School:

Indicators:

Students express an interest in advanced training in area of interest

Development of adolescent social interests may wane due to excessive involvement in area of interest

Intervention strategies:
Allow for time to be alone
Provide "shadowing" experiences
Avoid pressuring the student into social activities

Senior High:

Indicators:
Students become labeled in area of interest, e.g., "computer geek"
Has a desire to compete in area of interest
Expresses an interest in learning about how to pursue a career in area of interest

Intervention strategies:
Seek internship or paid work experiences
Talk to specialists in area of interest
Link with a mentor
Explore higher educational institutions that have a reputation in area of specialization

College:

Indicators:
Declares college major early
Seeks out mentors
Avoids many social interactions

Intervention strategies:
Explore areas of expression outside of academic curriculum, e.g., auditions, conventions
Link with a mentor

Pursue special areas of research or involvement
Consider graduate schools in area of interest

Those that are blessed with an extra dose of talent are often viewed as extremely self-reliant and independent. We're more likely to esteem them, envy them, or ignore them. Such presumptions are unfortunate. Like anyone, bringing out their best requires work, large doses of TLC, and our prayerful support.

It also requires a coordinated effort of support. Quite often, gifted-and-talented programs involve joint discussions of parents, teachers, special services specialists, and counselors. Meeting a few times each year, this support group approach creates, monitors, and adjusts an "Individual Development Plan" for the young person. By design and tradition, IDP's for gifted-and-talented students tend to be heavily biased in curriculum development (selecting courses) and creating special projects. Some provide special enrichment opportunities, such as visits to museums or touring art exhibits. Yet, more can and should be done to incorporate a measure of career awareness. Individual discussions with professionals, shadowing opportunities, or integrating a career component into course outlines will provide an intentionality to career planning that is absent in the majority of gifted and talented programs. If you're a parent of a gifted person, insist on it.

And then, one other requirement. As noted earlier, the plethora of interests that often accompanies multiple talents frequently yields one disheartening byproduct: confusion. Individual Development Plans (IDP's) should integrate a process that promotes decision-making skills. By fostering the skill of critical analysis with the awareness that "you can't have or do it all" will help. Such a process alleviates the bafflement that too often characterizes the careers—and lives—of adults who are gifted and talented. Insist on this, too.

Urban Persons of Color

We'll start this section with two questions.

Question #1: How many of you have been to the Magic Kingdom at Disneyworld or Disneyland?

Question #2: If you've been to either place, how many of you have journeyed on the ride called *It's a Small World*?

Probably, most of you. If you haven't, it's an around-the-world ride, featuring a chorus of doll-like figures who dance, sing, smile, and, of course, wear their traditional garb. The Japanese don their kimonos, the native Alaskans are bundled up in their furry coats, and the Dutch are klompin' in their wooden shoes.

There's something else going on while you're touring the continents. The song. While you're getting a taste of 120 cultures, you're hearing 120 versions of the same song. Although the languages vary, the tune is identical. What the Disney people don't tell you is that for the next five years minimum, you'll have that song bouncing around in your head. Only some heavy-duty deprogramming might rid you and your memory bank of that tune. I say *might*.

When that song and that ride were introduced thirty years ago, I doubt Disney knew how prophetic that tune would be. Doesn't it seem that with each successive year the world is indeed getting smaller? The "G" word—*global*—is becoming increasingly part of our daily vocabulary. As we become more global, there's another word that has entered our language. The "D" word: *diversity*. Diversity has surfaced traditions, lifestyles, and preferences that clearly distinguish us as peoples. In the same breath, those distinctions cause an odd blend of fascination and discomfort.

If we think this discussion about *diversity* is a passing fad, think again. Here is what's occurring:

- In 1995, 1/2 of children under age 5 in the U.S. were non-white.

- In 1994, the African American population was estimated to be 12.7% of the total population. By 2025, this segment of the population will likely represent 14%.
- The Hispanic population—10% of the total population in 1994—is projected to be 17% by 2025.
- The Asian population in the U.S. will more than double in the next 25 years to 25.5 million or 8% of the total.
- In 1993, only 53.1% of Hispanics in the United States over the age of 25 had completed high school or college, compared with 81% of Caucasians, and 70.4% of African Americans.

While most of these statistics witness a changing face to America, the latter statistic is perhaps the most revealing of all. If we can assume that educational attainment generally translates into a certain income level and accompanying standard of living, then it is no surprise that minorities, specifically Hispanics and African Americans, represent a disproportionate number in comparatively lower paying, service-oriented positions.

Therefore, a question. What can be done to underscore the importance of education for all cultures, which can serve as a means for a medley of other careers? And then, perhaps a more provocative and honest question: what can be done to eliminate the inherent biases of both the prevailing culture in our country as well as that of the particular culture of each ethnic group that will permit each *person*—not a *group*—to identify and exercise his or her imprint, their God-granted gifts and talents?

Perhaps, it first begins with certain perceived cultural standards of "expectation." Such expectations usually dictate a specific level of educational or career attainment. This seems to be particularly true for urban minorities. A frequent message in our urban centers is that "education" is not essential for making it in the world. Getting and keeping a *job* is the goal as opposed to choosing a *career*. Going beyond the high school diploma is often seen as an unnecessary waste of time and money. Long-range goals are frequently not a real part of urban minority families' schema. Perhaps, even more disheartening are the occasions where a young person shows real promise but it is suppressed by family pressure.

For many young, urban minorities, the "tribal village" concept may offer the highest impact, the most significant promise, and, unfortunately, the biggest threat. Members of the village or community can include the next-door neighbor, Grandma, the school counselor, the pastor, teachers, and one's parents. You simply can't underestimate how powerful their influence can be on a young person. Not surprisingly, however, it must begin with mom & dad.

As a "minority" in an otherwise dominant culture, there's a host of special challenges facing any young person. Many are overt; others rather subtle. Equipping a person with the affirmation—in other words, *encouraging* them—to dream is fundamental. It's not a one-time event either. It must transcend all activities, one's tone, and suggestions. Anything less diminishes the young person's self-esteem and consequently, their options.

Furthermore, as a person of color whose previous options might have been limited, it's a special challenge not to extend your own adolescent experience to that of your child. Yes, it'll prove awkward, particularly when seeing your child turned on to a possibility, a subject, or a career that is outside the norm. Any contrary response, no matter how small, can quickly generate feelings of rejection and guilt within your child. Not wanting to disappoint you, they'll often suppress or prevent those feelings by not pursuing their options, their dreams. They compromise. They lose, and we lose as a society. Don't allow this to happen by reminding yourself, checking yourself, expanding yourself.

If you're a person of color and a parent who possesses these feelings, you're not alone. Fortunately, a like-minded group of leaders, particularly in the Black community, have banded together to attack this phenomenon in an extraordinary initiative called the "Campaign for African- American Achievement." This group of leaders celebrates the achievements of scholars in a way that most schools honor athletes. In a series of ceremonies around the nation, thousands of young African-Americans have been inducted into the Thurgood Marshall National Achievers Society.

Here are a few suggestions to aid the career planning process, particularly if you're a parent of a minority young person in an urban environment:

- Stay close to your child's teacher and counselors. Talk to them about your child's progress. Learn what topics turn them on. Mutually brainstorm special projects that allow them to cultivate a special interest or skill.
- Attend Career Fairs or College Nights with your child
- Identify mentors. Mentors can be friends, Sunday School teachers, co-workers, community leaders, or coaches who can be both character mentors plus persons who can share information about their career. If it's difficult to identify such people, check with the school's counselor or principal. Or, suggest a historical or current personality whose walk is something to follow.
- Encourage your child to volunteer for a project or organization that parallels their interest and skills
- Develop a 30-day plan in which your child will conduct 3 "Information Interviews." These are conducted with persons who work in a field or actual position that might be of some interest to your child (see Appendix E for list of information interview questions)
- Get on the Web and check out sites that pertain to your child's interest
- Refer to the Ex Files chapter in this book for a complete list of activities you can either suggest or experience with your child.

Young Women

Where were you at 5:09 p.m. on November 30, 1980?

While you're probably racking your memory bank and speculating about what earth-shattering international event might have taken place, it was a time and date which proved eternal for me. It was the time that our first child, Ingrid, was born. Parents know these things.

Following a few minutes of some special bonding between new mom, dumbstruck dad, and our gorgeous baby, I left the delivery room to proclaim the great news. My in-laws immediately greeted me. I followed this exchange with a phone call to my parents, Ingrid's other brand-new grandparents. And those ecstatic conversations were followed with calls to other relatives, friends, and co-workers. My joyful shouts of "I'm a Dad!" came first. Then, came *the* question, "Is it a boy or a girl?"

It's a logical question. But, it's a question whose answer sets the wheels in motion—the wheels that will define how she'll behave and what she'll become—and all because of her gender and the *perceptions* we bring to that. Those perceptions play out in both subtle and pretty obvious ways. See if any of these contrasts sound familiar:

Girls	Boys
Barbie dolls	Tonka toys
ballet	wrestling
fiction	non-fiction
English	math & science
more passive	more aggressive
administrative assistant	chief executive officer
nurse	plumber
teacher	superintendent

At this very moment, some of you are taking a match—or a blowtorch—to this book. But hang tough with me for a moment. Believe me, it's not my intent to reinforce or advocate those contrasts but to point out the consequences of our traditions and assumptions. Please remember that

I was a new dad at that moment and only wanted all the best for my daughter. I still do.

Let's begin with an attempt to clarify the differences between girls and boys, at least in the context of learning, socialization, and career selection. Dr. Luther Otto, a research professor at North Carolina State University and director of the Career Development Study, offers three explanations for such differences:

- "Biological arguments reason that there are gender differences in personality that are fixed at conception, and that sex differences in occupational preferences are an expression of those innate biological determinants.
- Social structural explanations focus on discriminatory economic, political, and legal practices that deny equal opportunities to women in the workplace.
- Social learning explanations argue that people learn and acquire occupational preferences from others who, knowingly, or unknowingly, teach what society defines as 'appropriate' roles for men and women to aspire to and achieve."

As Moms and Dads, there's little we can do to influence the first two explanations; the last one, however, permits us some latitude and some direct participation. Again, Dr. Otto: "Parents can change some of the beliefs, values, and attitudes that hold young women back. Parents can manage the immediate learning environments in which their daughters grow up, and that gives parents a handle on at least part of the problem. Young women's career opportunities are affected—usually stifled—by the attitudes and behaviors others expect and that women learn and bring to the workplace. Of people with whom young women interact, none is more important than family and school."

Attitudes. Expectations. Behaviors. They start at home. They're also *managed* at home. So, let's pose a few hypothetical questions, particularly for those of you who are parents of daughters:

- To what degree, have you fostered the stereotypical feminine traits, e.g., being passive and deferring to others?
- How much have you encouraged your daughter to participate in competitive situations, contests, or sports?
- Do you envision your daughter aspiring to a top-level career position—in the same way you might forecast for your son?
- Do you have lesser expectations for your daughter in her math & science classes than in English or social studies?
- How do you talk about "women in the workplace" at home?
- Are you more prone to foster dependence or independence within your daughter?
- When your daughter is participating in an extracurricular activity, to what degree do you encourage her to pursue a leadership position in that group, club, or activity?
- How much "table talk" at home involves talking favorably about female role models?

These questions aren't intended to challenge your parental prerogative for how to raise your daughter. Nor, are they meant to make you feel guilty. What they reflect, however, are questions raised in society during the last three decades. The questions have led to decisions and a mindset that have altered the gender landscape with ramifications throughout society and certainly in the workplace.

They have also created opportunities. More young women, for instance, are entering college than ever before. And they're not just pursuing teaching, RN, or MRS degrees. There's evidence that women are breaking into traditionally macho jobs. As I pass by a new construction site, it's rare when I fail to see a female operating a front loader or pounding nails. In the last ten years, my community has seen women successfully perform as a CAD designer, Senior Vice-president, and minister.

Career Profile: **Sue Higgins, Public Administrator**

My parents strongly influenced my career selections mostly by their examples. My father is a very quiet, gentle man whose career goal was to be a doctor but who, largely because of financial realities, spent his working life as a supervisor at a floor machine company. He had a most effective way of being quite different from the average employee and still maintaining a widely held admiration. He refused to use profanity or participate in crude jokes, both of which were very common in his work environment. This example helped me build a strong belief that I did not have to fit any expected stereotype, no matter what career I selected.

My mother was a very strong influence in forming my personality as well as many of my career choices. She was one of the very first female officers in the Sheriff's Department in the early 50's. She did this without losing her warm and nurturing personality.

Above all, my parents provided excellent examples of pursuing their goals in their own ways. They each believed in living their own lives without feeling dictated by others' stereotypes. They didn't ridicule me when I stated that I knew there would be an old woman who would want me to have her harp (which did eventually happen) and they had strongly influenced my self-confidence in order to pursue my decision to change my career later in my life (from music to public administration). They provided excellent examples of down-to-earth reality mixed with enough courage to dream and challenge myself.

The break-throughs of women in the workplace may be attributed primarily to a newfound confidence rarely seen in history. Women are more assertive, self-confident, and competitive. They're more vocal and unabashed. They're not afraid to pound their stake in claim of territory. Yet, there's something to be said about swinging the pendulum too far, too fast. I find encouragement in the perspective of Dr. Luther Otto when he says, "I hope we can teach young women the importance of a competitive attitude, but I also hope women will maintain the traditional feminine values. As young women plan how they might storm the workplace Bastille and claim their fair share of the workforce, I also hope they will bring the feminine qualities of nurturance and caring with them. We'll all be the richer for it."

Yet, some continuing attention to these issues is necessary because the transformation doesn't come without a price. More specifically, the cost is in internal conflict. While women are anxious to aggressively enter the workplace, many of these same women are just as desirous of having children. Sooner or later, women ask the inevitable:

- To what degree, if at all, will my career be negatively affected if I have children?
- To what degree, if at all, will my kids be affected if I decide to work?
- If I want to have children, when is the "right" time?
- When my children are young, should I work full-time, part-time, or not at all?
- How are we going to maintain our standard of living if I don't work?
- If I take time out when having children, how difficult will it be for me to re-enter the workplace? How will others perceive me?

Fortunately, both employees and employers are working with women who desire both. Creative approaches, flexible hours, and work-at-home options are becoming more prevalent. Higher levels of flexibility are substituting traditional work mores without a compromise on competence and performance. One additional trend is emerging that promises even more opportunity to accommodate the wishes of work and family: women's use of technology and specifically, the Internet. By 1999, women surpassed men as users of the Internet, and they're extending their *use* into *leadership.* Carolyn Leighton, executive director of the 7,000 member professional group, *Women in Technology International,* says, "We now have wide-open opportunities where anyone can write the rules. And, I think we're going to see a major increase of women leadership because of that."

A prime example of such leadership by a woman in a technology-based business is Meg Whitman, CEO of the famed on-line auction site, *eBay.* At age 41, Ms. Whitman came to *eBay* where, within a year, she made the company one of the top 10 Internet businesses. Besides being CEO, she is a mother of two teenage sons and the wife of a brain surgeon. Says Ms. Whitman, "Virtually all of my time is dedicated to *eBay* and my family. It's a wonderful life."

Yet, a very important and compelling issue remains. With more and more women entering the workplace, what is the impact of working parents on kids? This is not to place the burden solely on women as working Moms. Yet, the issue has more poignancy now than ever before. Consequently, if the parents aren't parenting due to work, who or what is? Only time and research will tell. Perhaps, talking through these issues with your kids won't necessarily furnish the answers as much as it will help properly frame the questions.

In concluding this section, I have to confess that I was somewhat reluctant to even offer a portion on "Young Women" since the societal and occupational barriers are dissolving day-by-day. Some might claim that the differences are non-existent and, hence, a non-issue. As a parent of two daughters, I can be encouraged by such a claim, but in reality, differences exist and always will. After all, the good Lord made *two* sexes and not *one.* Acknowledging, adapting, and leveraging those differences offers each of us and our work environments a richer and more compelling experience.

Chapter VII

101 Ways to Partner With Your Child's School

It's Mitch's birthday! Normally, Mitch is pretty happy on his special day. But not this time. You see, this isn't just *any* birthday for Mitch. It's his 39th, a mere year from THE BIG FOUR-O.

When Mitch awakened on this particular day, he reflected on, well, certain bodily changes—changes like the hair missing from the top of his head that has now taken up residence in his ears. The spare tire that he had ten years ago has expanded to a full set of 4. Sound familiar? It just might—in more ways than one. In fact, you might have witnessed Mitch's lament a few years ago in the movie, *City Slickers,* featuring Billy Crystal. If you ever wanted to become educated about the predicaments and eccentricities associated with the male mid-life crisis, check it out. It's a classic.

Back to the movie's plot. By coincidence, Mitch's birthday coincides with "Career Day" for his teenage son, Danny. Danny's teacher feels hosting a couple of parents who would be willing to share their job experiences would benefit the occasion. The parent of a classmate of Danny's goes first. Then, it's Mitch's turn. Let's listen:

Mitch: *I work for WBLM radio.*

Teacher: *Are you a disc jockey?*

Mitch: *No, I'm not a disc jockey. You know all those commercials on the radio?*

Teacher: *Oh, do you make all those commercials?*

Mitch: *No, other people make the commercials. I sell them time on our station for the commercials to be on.*

Teacher: *So you decide which commercials will be on and when.*

Mitch: *That's right. Well, no. It's not right. It used to be right. It seems now I have to check with the station manager if I want to wipe my nose. The minute he took away my authority, I should have quit.* (Mitch pauses in contemplation for what seems an eternity and then continues.)

Value this time in your life kids because this is the time in your life when you still have all your choices. When you're a teenager, you think you can do anything, and you do. The twenties are a blur. The thirties are when you raise a family, make a little money, and you think, "What happened to my twenties?" (As Mitch is speaking, Danny is burying his head in his hands on his desk.)

The forties? You grow a little potbelly, you grow another chin, the music gets too loud, and your old girlfriend from high school becomes a grandmother. In your fifties, you have a minor surgery. You call it a "procedure." But, it's still a surgery.........

And so, the story—and Mitch's grumbling—continues for the sixties, the seventies, and the eighties. Don't adults say the darnest things?

When I first saw *City Slickers,* I wasn't sure whether I felt more sympathy for Danny, more embarrassment for his classmates, or genuine pity for his teacher. This will definitely be the teacher's very last effort at career education in her classroom. From now on, nothing but algebra problems and spelling tests.

Unfortunately, the level of career awareness for many students is little more than we just encountered from Billy Crystal. OK, maybe a bit more. 8th graders often take a standardized career assessment. There might be the occasional field trip to the largest employer in town. Or, 3rd graders might do a 100-word essay on "What I Want to be When I Grow Up." Most of us have been there, right?

School systems might want to take note, however. In a 1994 Gallup survey, respondents said that schools are not doing enough career development for both the college-bound and employment-bound students, particularly the non-college bound students. Here are a few other conclusions from that study:

- 75% of non-college bound students feel schools are not doing enough for them.
- Two-thirds of adults contend that schools should do more to assist dropouts and graduates in job skill training and job search skills.
- Two-thirds of high school students believe schools are not doing enough in career preparation.
- More than 50% of adults advocate greater assistance by schools in developing job-seeking skills.

Lest we put all the blame on schools, some understanding is required for the changing roles of teachers and guidance counselors. Increasingly, teachers are compelled to wear multiple hats: surrogate parent, nutritionist, disciplinarian, family mediator, classroom arbitrator, and, oh yeah, facilitator of knowledge. It's just as difficult for school counselors who usually live by the 90/10 rule. 90% of their time is spent on 10% of the students, and those students are either the extremely talented or extremely troubled. Student load is another problem for counselors. It's not uncommon for counselors to handle 500-600 students, making it nearly impossible to get to know most students' academic or career plans, let alone their names.

And then there's the matter of preparation. How or when do student teachers receive instruction during college on ways of integrating career education into their daily lesson plans? It's rare, at best. Consequently, most teachers follow the pattern of what they experienced when they were elementary or high school students. Yeah, *City Slickers* may be more truth than fantasy.

Certainly, there's the potential for more. Much more. By means of a combined and particularly creative initiative between the community, parents, and teachers, career development can and must achieve greater significance.

The community can serve as a major player. Its members can include social service agencies, units of government, the arts, health care institutions, churches, and businesses. Their assistance can range from providing dollars or volunteering time. From the perspective of those in the business sector, it simply makes good business sense. As employers continually require a technically and socially prepared workforce, it's prudent to stay in one's own backyard and cultivate the next generation of employees. Exposing young people to the range of career choices in their places of business is fundamental.

While businesses and other community participants are helpful, *true* participation and involvement in the schools can best be derived from the home. From you. Teachers covet your tangible support and ideas, particularly when it comes to the uncharted territory of career development. Your offer of assistance to your child's teacher or his or her school will be considered as a genuine gift from heaven. Prepare for sainthood, lavish gifts, and inexhaustible praise.

So, the simple question: how? OK, let's take out the *simple* part, and ask what is any one way that you, as a parent, can help with career preparation at school? Rather than one way, let's consider *101* ways that you might assist.

The following list is a menu of such possibilities. You'll quickly discern that some ideas require direct and active involvement. Others are occasional, at best. Some involve a joint effort with other parents, teachers, or school officials. Similar to the "Ex-Files" chapter, each idea is accompanied by a suggested school level.

Well, the choices are yours. They simply require your initiative in offering your assistance, some time, and your creativity.

<u>Scale</u>

L = Lower elementary grades (1-3)
U = Upper elementary grades (4-5)
M = Middle school grades (6-8)
S = Senior High School (9-12)

1. Job shadowing—Students observe an employee or working parent for a full or partial day at the worksite (L, U, M, S)
2. Presentations—Working adults, parents, or representatives of different occupations offer a description or demonstration of their career to a group of students at school (L, U, M, S)
3. Interactive field trips—Students assist in preparing the field trip itself, participating in it, and then reflecting on it either orally or in writing (U, M, S)
4. Community interviews—Individual students or groups of students meet various people in the community and conduct interviews, using a standard interview/question format (M, S)
5. Summer work experiences for teachers—Teachers volunteer to engage in a full or partial Summer program by working in manufacturing or service sector setting with the intention of enhancing their curriculum through non-teaching work assignments and projects. (U, M, & S teachers)
6. Career focus conferences—Schools focus on a specific career field, e.g., humanities, technology, and these conferences for the purpose of learning about career opportunities consistent with the discipline. One conference, for instance, could emphasize engineering opportunities. Such a conference could be held at a research and design center. (S)

7. Career day—One day each semester or year would be devoted to highlighting the "World of Work." (L, U, M, S)
8. Daily bulletins about career-related issues and trends should be posted in classrooms or by the counseling offices. (M, S)
9. On-line—Every student needs instruction about how to use the computer for career planning and job search skills. (L, U, M, S)
10. Project Sessions—12-20 students come to a organization or a business to complete a project or conduct a work simulation. (S)
11. Develop Career Conferences around multiple intelligences (M, S)
12. Participate in Decision-Making lesson plans by hosting parents who answer these questions (M, S):
    A. How did you make a decision about your career?
    B. If you could do it all over, how would you adjust your decision-making process?
13. At the conclusion of each major unit, semester, or course have each student answer the following questions (S—both teachers and parents):
    A. What were the top 3 things you learned during this course?
    B. What did you learn about yourself?
    C. What careers are associated with the focus of this class?
    D. Which one(s), if any, interest you? What will you do now to learn more about them?
14. Post the "Daily Bulletins" from *Bridges.com* (an on-line career planning web-site) about job trends, job descriptions, career testimonies, etc. Area businesses might underwrite this program within a school. (S)
15. Junior Achievement—Students in grades K-12 learn economic concepts from by engaging in start-up businesses. Area business people providing coaching and mentoring under the auspices of this nationally recognized program. (S)
16. Robots Project—Promising engineering students work in tandem with area engineers, tool & die makers, electricians, etc. to construct

an actual robot that is entered into competition. This after school project serves as a valuable learning tool. (S)

17. Science Fairs—Physics, chemistry, geology, biology, and computer science students construct science projects that are evaluated and judged by working professionals in their respective disciplines. (U, M, S)
18. Sponsor a "Top Ten Hot Jobs" Day with speakers representing each field. (S)
19. Develop a program called "How Not to Have Another B-O-R-I-N-G Summer." Outline low-cost activities that offer new opportunities for career awareness. (S)
20. Take a field trip to the Resource Center or Guidance Office to learn more about their "Careers" section (S)
21. Require a visit to the Career or Tech Center (S)
22. Develop a Parent Newsletter that highlights various career-related topics, including (S)
    A. Exciting Opportunities That Don't Require a College Degree
    B. This Job Isn't What You Think It Is! (a parent describes his/her job)
    C. Dual Career Couples
23. Encourage working persons to run for school boards or participate on committees where career awareness can and should be an important theme or emphasis.
24. Area businesses can offer scholarships or compensation for teachers to work part-time or during the summer in a professional environment that will enhance their curriculum.
25. Develop 3-year partnerships between a school and an organization/business. Specific themes can apply to each year. Activities should also occur between teachers and the organization's employees, not simply between the students and members of the organization's human resources department (L, U, M, S)

26. Create Kidpreneurship or youth enterprise programs. It's a junior version of Junior Achievement. (L, U, M)
27. Have employees tutor at-risk students. While focusing on reading or computational skills, such mentoring offers opportunities to discuss the career of the tutor. (L, U, M, S)
28. Parents should encourage school districts to access School-to-Work federal funds, providing meaningful ways for non-college bound students to pursue technical careers.
29. Businesses provide contributions (financial, materials, equipment, in kind) to schools. (L, U, M, S)
30. Businesses design and construct replica operations, such as an assembly operation, test lab, or quality lab, or design department in school. The furnishing of this equipment is supplemented by occasional instruction or examples of how the equipment is used in the workplace. (S)
31. Offer scholarships to graduating seniors with the stipulation that they work for the sponsoring organization part-time during the school year or during summers (S)
32. Have a local professional organization sponsor a school with activities and goals similar to a typical business/education partnership. (L, U, M, S)
33. Have a local professional organization speak to students, counselors, and teachers about scholarships offered by their profession. (S)
34. Create an educational/business interactive group, involving solely superintendents or principals and CEO's from area businesses to discuss issues of common interest at *their* level.
35. Have the local Chamber or State Employment office publish and distribute job forecasts to area teachers. (M, S)
36. When talking about real-world problems, bring in an adult expert in that field to lend an up-close-and-personal perspective on the issue(s). (M, S)

37. Have adults come in to discuss core competencies (public speaking, writing, decision- making, team work) and how they use them in the workplace. Link a specific area with a current item in the teacher's lesson plan (S)
38. Create *Individual Development Plans* for each student, beginning with middle school. IDP's are intended to identify specific learning objectives, special activities, or specifically required resources for the student's development at the beginning of each school year. In order to maintain a level of career awareness, each IDP should involve 3 information interviews each year. (M, S)
39. Have students link with an adult in a volunteer capacity. Service to one's community begins with early experiences. (M, S)
40. Students too young to be employed can take on a "minimal" job role, doing jobs around the house or for a neighbor. Constructive feedback and tons of affirmation works wonders. (U, M)
41. Following career assessments that are common in middle school, each student should conduct 2-3 information interviews in the occupations that were identified. (M)
42. Have minorities, females, and/or disabled persons address students on career options and formulas for success. (M, S)
43. Sponsor field trips to the primary facets of the community (manufacturing, educational, service). If necessary, investigate whether sponsoring organizations might be willing to pick up the tab for transportation expenses. (M, S)
44. The *Choices* Program—*Choices* addresses mother/daughter issues related to career development. 6-12 pairs of moms and their children meet weekly at each other's homes. During the 90-minute sessions, they work through the activities in *Choices.* A similar book is available for boys called, *Challenges.* (S)
45. Parent Nights—Three evenings throughout the year are featured in which topics, such as assessment, career planning, course selection, job seeking, and financial aid are presented. Both students

and their parents attend with time devoted to plot individual strategies. Make special efforts to highlight careers that are nontraditional to one's gender. (S)

46. Parent Interviews—parents and students attend an evening program in which students rotate to five other parents for mini-presentations about their careers. (S)
47. Create an inter-generational panel of recent grads, parents, and grandparents that discuss how careers and career patterns have changed. (S)
48. Participate in a local or regional Peer Review Committees composed of local business and education representatives. Their primary purpose is to review programs and ensure compliance with the career competency standards in tandem with other evaluation criteria. Future state funding of programs is contingent upon addressing peer review findings.
49. Create a panel of young, single mothers to discuss ways of parenting, childcare, and careers. (S)
50. Sponsor a bi-monthly "Career Awareness Day" that highlights careers through presentations of various parts of the community (health, criminal justice, economic development, education, religious life, the arts, government, etc.) (L, U, M, S)
51. Bring in adult speakers with relevant experiences or knowledge of current local, national, or international events. (M, S)
52. Piggy-back on special speakers to local service organizations or a nearby college by having them speak informally to groups of students about both a topic in their area of expertise but also about their career, the required training, pros & cons, and the employability potential of their career. Focus on small, informal groups that facilitate interaction between the speaker and the students. (M, S)

53. Coaches of middle school or high school sports could talk from their experience about sports-related careers and how sports has affected their personal and professional lives. (M, S)
54. School clubs could sponsor a speaker to discuss careers in an area of interest, a mini-"Career Night," job shadowing, or a field trip to location that reflects the club's interest (M, S)
55. Although not directly career-focused, volunteer programs, such as "Kids' Hope," get adults and parents into the school setting and provide excellent interaction between students and adults. These programs are oriented toward at-risk children and focus on literacy, math skills, and appropriate behaviors. Invariably, some discussion about the adult's vocation or career planning will occur. (L, U)
56. In an effort to address the critical needs for more electrical engineers and most positions in the IT industry, Texas Instruments is working with school districts in the Dallas, Texas area. They are specifically introducing algebraic concepts to students much earlier (prior to 8th grade) which enhances a student's understanding of algebra—a key subject area in information technology. TI speaks to both students about practical applications of algebra and meets with teachers to offer suggestions about how to enhance the curriculum through "real world" applications. Perhaps, a local business in your area could initiate a similar program. (M)
57. To assist teachers in understanding computers, Intel, Microsoft and Hewlett-Packard co- sponsor the ACE Academy, a two-week program that familiarizes teachers with technology. It demonstrates ways that computers can be integrated into the classroom and the workplace, recognizing that 65% of all current jobs require workers to possess high-tech skills. If not available in your community, school districts or a consortium of similar industries might develop a similar program. (L, U, M, S)

58. Toward the end of the 12th grade, a student's portfolio is reviewed by a committee of school staff and business representatives/parents to determine if the student is eligible for a *Certificate of Employability.* This certificate is a product of commendable performance in the areas of core academics, applied learning competencies, attendance, and citizenship. (S)
59. Establish a self-directed career center for use by both students *and* parents with appropriate hours for both parties and available year-round. (S)
60. Develop a parent/educator-developed web site, informing parents and residents about school programs, particularly about career-related issues, such as Tech Prep and School-to-Work initiatives, upcoming speakers, Career Nights, or career-related resources. (S)
61. Patterned after a program from Broadalbin-Perth High School in New York, create an evening program titled, *Parents as Partners,* that targets technical careers requiring no more than a two-year degree. Try to have as many parents serve as presenters or hosts of booths during the evening. (S)
62. Create and send a *Parent Handbook* sent to all parents of senior high students, including articles, essays, and recommendations from parents. Highlight opportunities available for the employment-bound students. (S)
63. Have PTO (Parent-Teacher Organizations/Associations) participants personally invite a friend to attend an upcoming PTO meeting. PTO/PTA's are excellent forums for school improvement and information. The more parents are able to attend these programs, the better. (L, U, M, S)
64. Identify a career-related topic and appropriate presenter as the featured topic at a PTO/PTA meeting. (L, U, M, S)
65. Recognizing that healthy financial planning begins early in life, identify a parent of a child within the school who is a licensed/certified financial planner or an investments counselor who can discuss

with students the importance of personal finances. Sub-topics in this area can include savings, budgeting, salaries & wages of various occupations, retirement, and investments. (S)

66. Invite a member of the local State Employment Commission to come in and discuss their services and job trends in the immediate area at a teachers' meeting, PTO/PTA meeting, a high school Government class, or a workshop on "Job Readiness." (S)
67. Host a "Work Experience Day" that highlights part-time jobs in the area. A large area, such as a gym or multi-purpose room, would include displays from area organizations that students could visit and talk to representatives. Begin the program with a description on the merits, challenges, and issues associated with part-time employment and the need to maintain balance with the studies. (S)
68. Identify recent alumni who have either 1) graduated from high school and are in the workplace, and 2) graduated from college and are now working. Have them share some "Workplace Realities" and offer advice to currents students on career and academic preparation. (S)
69. Sponsor a "Community Services Day" in which professionals, para-professionals, and volunteers (ideally, parents of students) share a description of their respective service organizations, such as Habitat for Humanity or the American Red Cross) plus an explanation of their role, their background, and any other pertinent information. Students could also have an opportunity to sign-up as a volunteer for the organization of their choice. (M, S)
70. Have area IT industries, consulting firms, and businesses sponsor an "IT Event," which focuses on emerging IT careers. Representatives of these careers discuss their occupation and conduct IT "show-and-tell" demonstrations of the latest hardware and software. (M, S)

71. Whether you call them *Terrific Tuesdays, Wonderful Wednesdays,* or *Fabulous Fridays,* these lunch-time programs for elementary children are great ways to acquaint them with different careers. These programs are typically several weeks long, are highly interactive, and frequently led by parents of students. Rather than a lecture about a specific occupation, these "hands-on" programs teach a skill, craft, or activity that is common to the career of the facilitator. (L, U)
72. Often labeled as HOSTS (Helping One Student To Succeed) or "The Dream Team," a group of employees from a business take it upon themselves to work with an at-risk child. The adults work with the child on life and academic skills. The actual tutoring and facilitation often occurs at the workplace instead of the child's school. Tours of the facility, related-internships, or presentations on the Job-of-the-Month provide opportunities for the student(s) to learn either directly or indirectly about various careers. (U, M, S)
73. School administrators or a PTO can create a database about the careers of the students' parents. When completing the initial form that asks for this information, parents can indicate their interest in speaking to a class or a student about his/her occupation. (L, U, M, S)
74. Since the schedules of working parents may make it difficult to participate in many of the activities and functions listed here, teachers should consider grandparents or retirees. Their perspective can often be nothing short of fascinating.
75. As a parent, a great way to create interaction between your child and some working professionals is by taking them to a community service function, such as a Rotary Club, Kiwanis Club, Chamber of Commerce, or church function. Not only will they meet other adults, but they are likely to hear a special speaker. It's helpful to obtain a list about the topics of upcoming speakers in order to

pick a subject of possible interest for your child. These opportunities are excellent opportunities for adults to share some information about their occupations. And they serve as simple and subtle ways to kick-off some solid networking opportunities! Make things even better by inviting your child's teacher. (U, M, S)

76. Invite a local TV or radio personality to speak to your child's class on the importance of communication, English, marketing, and specific traits that make for success. That person could be accompanied by another person from the station in an important supportive role (program manager, technician, engineer, etc.), highlighting other less glamorous but still very important and interesting positions that are critical to the station's operations. (M, S)

77. Local, county, State, and even national political candidates rely heavily on young people to assist them in their campaigns. The two major political parties sponsor Youth Campaign committees to canvas, organize, make phone calls, send out mailings, and perform other functions. Significant interaction with other like-minded adults provides opportunities to learn about other careers and to establish networks. Contact your community's political parties to learn of such opportunities. (S)

78. Many schools conduct an "Information Night" for each grade level that is intended solely for parents. The program often consists of discussion about attendance, school behavior, dates of parent/teacher conferences, etc. Principals, teachers, and counselors should also outline their approach on the inclusion of career-related topics in the curriculum and elsewhere in the school. (M, S)

79. A common strategy for fostering business-education relationships is through a one-to-one partnership between a school and a designated business. The extent of the relationship can range from occasional exchanges to frequent and in-depth activities. Employees from the sponsoring business could make presentations about their

respective careers. Field trips are very educational. Other activities include social functions, job shadowing, and mini-career fairs. Occasionally, teachers serve a summer internship at the sponsoring organization. (L, U, M, S)

80. Enlisting a professional athlete to speak to a group of students or an entire school can be entertaining, inspiring, and educational. It can also be tremendously clarifying. Many young people live with the illusion of becoming a pro athlete someday. Odds of ever getting drafted for a professional career are a startling .002. Rather, pro athletes can advocate the merits of self-discipline, perseverance, and teamwork—qualities that are relevant for any career. (U, M, S)

81. A standard for many career assessments is the *Self-Directed Search* instrument developed by Dr. John Holland. It links six different personality "types" with various careers. After taking and scoring the test, students could hear career presentations from parents that reflect each of the six types. (M, S)

82. A promising and lucrative alternative for many students is participation in a certified apprenticeship program. Working adults (preferably, parents) could make presentations to students about their career as a journeyman in a designated trade. Such presentations are extremely helpful in clarifying common stereotypes of trades people while outlining the typically excellent job prospects in most skilled trades. (S)

83. We started this book with a story about "Take Your Daughter to Work Day." How could we forget this important day that served as a vital catalyst for many young women? Thankfully, the day has expanded for young men to join either their moms or dads. While this designated day usually involves shadowing, tours, and, of course, having lunch, many organizations develop rather elaborate programs with mini-sessions on career planning, technology, and some hands-on activities. (L, U, M, S)

84. Career Roundtables—Typically intended for senior high school students, these mini-forums are one-hour Q & A sessions on diverse career opportunities in the area. Local firms send reps to talk about careers within their organizations. For instance, one of our area high schools annually has a person from H & R Block, the tax people, encourage young people to consider careers as tax preparers. To foster interaction and attendance, Roundtables are often held in school cafeterias or Resource/Media Centers. (S)
85. Develop a business/education partnership between a school and a particular business that focuses on:
    A. The problem-solving techniques that the business uses
    B. A discussion of "real world" issues as experienced in business
86. Communities might consider the creation of "magnet" schools that concentrate on a particular discipline, such as the fine arts or math & science. Objectives of these schools include:
    A. Advancing students' knowledge well beyond standard courses
    B. Providing students with a rich assortment of advanced placement and honors program
    C. Offering opportunities for students to utilize higher-level thinking
    D. Encouraging students and teachers to learn from practicing professionals in the business community. (S)
87. Encourage students to maintain an Individual Career Plan (ICP). This plan is kept in a folder with space for a student, student's job-related experiences, self-assessments, resumes, and any insights or relevant materials throughout high school. During the student's senior year, this ICP is reviewed between a teacher of the student's choosing, and a member of the community consistent with the student's career interest. (S)
88. Whenever and if appropriate, provide opportunities for students to serve on school committees, Boards of Education, or ad hoc committees that involve teachers, administrators, and parents.

Such interaction allows students to engage in real world issues, to contribute a student's perspective, to network with other parents, and to either directly or indirectly learn about other occupations. (S)

89. Student newspapers are ALWAYS looking for articles. Encourage the newspaper's editor to consider having a regular entry called something like *Career Corner* or *Just About Jobs* that feature articles about local employers, employment trends, careers of students' parents, etc. Perhaps, the parents themselves might be willing to compose an article. (S)

90. Sponsor a "Lunch & Learn" program whereby each month students can learn about a specific career field from an area professional or from a parent. To encourage attendance, the school could offer freebies: ice cream, soda, popcorn, etc. Sorry, only kids can attend. (S)

91. Human Resources managers (or an area association of HR professionals) can conduct mock interviews for high school students in job readiness classes. (S)

92. Parents whose careers deal with international business can come to high school foreign language classes and speak about careers in international business or positions with the State department. Even respective State governments are creating positions to lure foreign investment. Related discussions could occur about the importance of studying other cultures. (S)

93. High school counselors or PTO's might create a "Former Graduate Career Speakers Bureau" that is a data base of graduates willing to speak in any class (and, of course, based on their availability) about their current career. Alumni could speak about use of technology, training/education, pay rates, etc., as they pertain to their jobs. (S)

94. As an alternative to the former suggestion (# 93), an English, Journalism, or Media class could take on a project that compiles

the career profiles of several alumni. Brief testimonials about their career, use of technology, job growth, pay rates, etc. could be common elements for each of the profiles. The collection could be developed in print, video, or CD-ROM format. (S)

95. Either on a "Career Day" or as part of a class dealing with career planning, create a Scavenger Hunt in which small groups (4-6 students) must investigate, talk to, and take pictures of six different occupations (matching Dr. Holland's RIASEC career/personality typology). It's a blast to accomplish the Scavenger Hunt in one day and report on it. If not, spread the task over a week or two. Since transportation is a must for this task, middle school students will require some giving parents to assist with the driving. High school students can do this on their own (with school and parental approval). (M, S)

96. Our local Chamber of Commerce annually honors an individual as a "Small Business Person of the Year." The ceremony announcing and honoring the individual occurs at a special breakfast meeting. The attendance at this breakfast is one of the largest events of the year. Students from area schools could be invited to this meeting, which could be followed by a separate session between the honoree and the students. This session could discuss not only the person's specific occupation, but the traits that led to his/her success. (M, S)

97. When my brother was a 7th grader, he already had an avid interest in flying and was interested in starting a Flying Club. Fortunately, a junior high science teacher possessed his private flying license and was game to be the faculty advisor. I often wonder what would have happened to my brother's interest in flying (he eventually earned his Bachelor's degree in Aviation) if such a teacher hadn't stepped forward. As an option, parents can assume this role and serve as an *adult advisor* for various school clubs and organizations. (M, S)

98. With the increasing use of video conferencing and e-mail, schools can link with individuals worldwide to learn more about various careers. The use of this technology could be particularly beneficial, informative, and fascinating when talking to well-known personalities, such as an actor, astronaut, athlete, or diplomat. (U, M, S)
99. When your Congressman, Senator, or State Representative is in the area, he or she could address a government class for the purpose of discussing careers in public service. (M, S)
100. When sponsoring a high school commencement speaker, schools can make a day out of it by hosting the speaker in a series of discussion groups, including one that addresses the speaker's particular career and how they were influenced to do what they do. (S)
101. On one day each year, a group of students in a photojournalism class could focus (sorry!) on persons in a variety of careers as they perform their jobs. Upon displaying their photographs, each student should share one element that reinforced their perception of the career plus one item that was significantly different from their expectation. (S)

So, which one do you want to do? Which one makes sense in your child's school? Maybe, you should ask your child. There's probably at least one idea that sounds pretty cool to them. Whatever idea you decide upon, just make it happen. Let me encourage you to zero in on one idea and make a call to your child's teacher or school principal by the end of the week.

There's one more suggestion that I failed to list. You might have someone come in to talk about "The Future of Jobs & Jobs of the Future." In fact, *you* could be that someone. It's actually a piece of cake. All the material for your speech is in the next chapter. In no time, you'll be on the speaking circuit, bringing down $10,000 per speech, and being escorted in limos.

Just remember who gave you the goods.

Chapter VIII

The Future of Jobs and Jobs of the Future

His pocket watch said 2:50 a.m. on this chilly February night in Liverpool in 1817. Henry had less than ten minutes to get to his appointed designation, the Remington Mills Company. Yes, it would be pitch-black en route, but that wouldn't pose a problem. He knew the route like the back of his hand. After all, he had done it for the last 23 years, every day of the week but Sundays. He started working at Remington the day he turned thirteen.

This middle-of-the-night trip to work was different, however. Threateningly different. At 3 a.m., he'd meet with a band of 60 other workers to do the unthinkable: destroy a half-dozen new, steam-driven wool-finishing machines at Remington. If he got caught, it would cost him a lot more than just his job. A 25-year prison term would be guaranteed.

For Henry, however, the prospect of jail didn't deter him. The target of their search-and-destroy mission was a genuine threat to his trade and that of his colleagues. Three months ago, Remington had purchased these new high-tech wonders that allegedly could produce as much as four or five people. Not only were they quicker, but also some said they made products less expensively. Even better. But, you wouldn't convince Henry about these things.

He dashed out his bungalow and within minutes met up with his fellow employees, now marauders. Within seconds they were in the shop. With sledgehammers and crowbars, they set about their task with a vengeance. It took less than five minutes to accomplish their mission, escape, and scatter undetected. Henry was back in bed by 3:30 a.m., and no one knew the difference—at least, until the morning's light and the arrival of Remington's first shift.

What Henry and company performed that winter's night was not without precedent in 1817, however. All over southern England, the hub of the milling industry, similar raiding parties were waging war against their employers. A common bond was promptly created for these crews under the label of "Luddites" after a mythical leader, General Ned Ludd.

For nearly fifteen months, these roving bands battled technology. But, eventually, the efforts of Henry and his colleagues proved futile. Surprisingly, it wasn't Great Britain's version of the FBI that did them in. It was something more potent: the power of consumer demand. The British in the early 19th century simply liked what they saw: cheaper and higher quality products. And all because of technology. As much as Henry and his fellow Luddites treasured the status quo, their unwillingness to recognize and embrace change led to their demise, leaving them little more than an occasional reference in a history book.

Remnants of Luddites still exist today, however. Those that resemble contemporary "Luddites" will be severely hampered, abandoned, or, at worst, lost. Our new century will have little similarity to any of the previous ones, even with the last decade of the 20th. While many changes will be appear to be far-fetched and fictional, the changes will be very real, rampant, and profound.

Perhaps, no other aspect of our society will experience as much significant change as in the work place. Work environments and how people pursue their careers will be different. Dramatically different. Prompting those changes are societal fluxes, demographic changes, and technological advances. How those changes will play out in terms of opportunities are subject to speculation, yet this is indisputable: the future of jobs and job of the future will be unlike anything we've ever experienced or imagined.

The remainder of this chapter will briefly examine these changes with a focus on these elements:

- Societal and demographic changes
- How "work" will be performed
- Required traits of the new worker
- Jobs of the future

Those of you who are "Luddites" will likely find the following information discomforting. "Change agents" will sense excitement and anticipation. For them, the play can't begin soon enough.

A Slower, More Diverse, and Less Loyal Workforce

Perhaps, no other book is the defined leader for career information than the *Occupational Outlook Handbook,* a bi-annual publication from the Department of Labor. In an effort to frame forthcoming changes in both careers and the workplace, the editors of this book have written the following: *Opportunities result from the relationships between the population, labor force, and the demand for goods and services. Population ultimately limits the size of the labor force—individuals working or looking for work—which constrains how much can be produced.* Kind of sounds like something from a less-than-thrilling textbook in Econ 101.

OK, assuming the editors' premise is true, the production of goods and services and more specifically, the *kinds* of goods and services, will vary due to changes in demographics. Here's a sampling of some population shifts plus some changes in the composition of the workforce as offered in the *Occupational Outlook Handbook* and their sources of information, the Bureau of Labor Statistics (BLS).

- The BLS projects that the labor force will grow to 14.9 million between 1996 and 2006 and this is 1.2 million less than the previous

10 years, reflecting slower growth in the civilian population 16 years of age and older.

- The number of self-employed workers is expected to increase to 11.6 million by 2006.
- The labor force growth of Hispanics, Asians, and other races will be faster than for Blacks and non-white Hispanics due to immigration.
- Between 1996 and 2006, women's share of the labor force will grow to 47 percent, reflecting a trend that began in 1976.
- In the first decade of the 21st century, age groups with large numbers of Baby Boomers will grow by more than 30 percent—people 45 to 54 and those 55 to 64.
- The 25 to 34 year old age group will decline by 3.0 million, a result of falling birth rates in the late 1960's.
- The contingent and temporary work force is expected to grow 1.5 times faster than other employment between 2000 and 2009.
- In 2000, part-time, temporary, and self-employed workers represented 33% of the civilian work force.

The consequences of all these changes and shifts will be mostly welcomed in the marketplace. More dual career families translate into higher earnings and more discretionary income. New and different goods and services will fuel an ever-growing economy.

Yet, not everything will come up roses. Most ominous in the above data will be a shrinking labor force. Equally foreboding is a shortage of skilled labor. Not only are basic literacy skills at question, but also the necessary skill levels for most technical positions will be lacking. Our country continues to experience 700,000 high school dropouts each year, and the supply of skilled talent in manufacturing and technical areas is decreasing. We'll pay for these declines with our pocket books and in the quality of our goods. And, if we can't satisfy our wants in a way that we want them and at a decent price, guess who's waiting just outside our territorial limits? Is it any wonder that our balance of trading continues to go from bad to worse? If there ever was a time to establish a national policy that addresses educational standards, skill preparation, and a global trade policy, it's now. Our standard of living depends on it.

Fortunately, many institutions and segments in society are taking up the cause. It's perhaps most notable in the work place where the old profit motive—in the face of global competition—is requiring work to be performed in vastly different ways. The next section tells us how.

The Changing Nature of Work

The alarm goes off at 7:50 a.m. Kate has just enough time to brush her teeth, turn the coffee pot on, and battle the daily commute to work which today, as with most days, begins at 8 a.m. She once calculated that her commute from the coffee pot to her work was a distance of 22. That's steps, not miles.

Yes, you read right. Kate, like an increasing number of individuals, is a telecommuter. Her work begins with the flick of a switch: the computer switch. Once it's on and in operation, she's ready to roll. Her agenda includes an 8:15 a.m. teleconference meeting (she has just enough time to put a brush through her hair) with colleagues in Tokyo, Columbus, and Fort Worth. She'll look over the financials from the previous month courtesy of headquarters. And, in the afternoon, she'll prepare a Power Point presentation that she'll deliver to a customer next month. Well, she won't personally deliver it; her computer will.

Sound far-fetched? It's anything but. Increasingly, independent contractors plus regular employees of small and large corporations consider this schedule their daily fare. The "what" of work hasn't changed all that much—just the "how." Here's a list of other changes that are forever changing the nature of work:

- Organizations won't be "organized." The Nineties witnessed the collapse of the "formal" organization with its multiple layers of management. In the next 20 years, the sacred labels of "manager" and "employee" may be anachronisms. In its wake, new organizations may be defined as a "blended" workforce composed of these groups.

- A core group of employees at the top of the organization whose primary role is articulating a strategic direction.
- A full-time, well-educated group of knowledge workers whose job is project and team management in support of the strategic goals.
- Contingent workers and consultants who participate on teams and projects, exercising their particular area of expertise. Such persons may be working on multiple assignments in several companies simultaneously.
- Technicians who know how to operate and service the advanced computer equipment. Technology will permit them to conduct most of their work from their home office.
- Third party organizations that assume specific functions within an organization. Companies will outsource various functions due to their expertise, economy of scale, and price. Examples of such functions could be, if they're not already, food service, benefits administration or the maintenance of office supplies.
- Compensation will be radically different. Annual cost-of-living adjustments will be lost and gone forever. They'll be substituted by variable pay systems that directly reflect an individual's or a team's ability to provide tangible value. "Value" will be determined by speed to market, speed of delivery, quality, and cost savings. In other words, performance. No longer will individuals receive rewards for their efforts toward achieving goals or by the number of people one manages. Instead, the individual's actual bottom-line contributions will translate into compensation and future opportunities. The same holds true for all groups in organization, even contingent workers and third party groups.
- Since "performance" will become an operative word for all employees and participating groups, feedback will become more frequent,

specific, and spontaneous. Mediocrity won't be tolerated for long. Performance appraisals will focus on goal achievement and team-based behavior.

- Teamwork will be everywhere. Self-managed work teams will be assembled for the purpose of interacting more frequently with customers and satisfying their expectations. Often, those teams will be comprised of vendors, suppliers, the customers themselves, and even competitors! Work will become more project-oriented with employees migrating in and out of teams based on their particular specialty or expertise.
- No more gold watches. Company loyalty will become a long-lost tradition as employees remove the embroidered name off their Polo shirt and substitute it with "Free Agent." Labor attorney, Martin F. Payson, says, "There will be less loyalty to the organization because people will be more wedded to the product they make, the service they perform, or the technology they use than the company they work for."
- Education won't be a personal chapter that ends with commencement exercises in high school or college. Life-long learning will be the norm. Consider this: much of a fresh college graduate's knowledge base will be obsolete within 5 years of their degree. In order to stay competitive, training and education budgets for companies will total in the billions, not millions of dollars. Changes in technology, access to information, and dissatisfaction with the current K-12 system are escalating these costs. Lawrence Sherr, a Chancellors' Club distinguished professor at the University of Kansas School of Business cites Motorola's efforts at education. He indicates, "Right now, Motorola is investing close to $100 million in education for its employees. Businesses are waking up to the fact that society is not doing the job in education. They'll have to do it themselves."

- In connection with a discussion about education, the norm of equating college degrees with financial success may be altered. The emphasis will be on what persons actually know and what is a marketable competency. Certificates of study that focus on a particular area of knowledge, skill, or technology will become more popular and desired.
- We're just beginning to see the tip of the iceberg on on-line education and distance learning. Education will be from campuses-without-walls, allowing learning to occur in the privacy of one's home or office. On-line chat groups will replace the traditional classroom. Even bastions of traditional education, such as the Ivy League schools, will enlist this new format.
- Like Kate in the above story, telecommuting may become the career of choice. It's already evident as telecommuting from home grew by 89% between 1991 and 1997. Telecommuting offers flexibility, particularly for persons wanting to balance their personal and work lives. Home offices will become increasingly popular and inviting. After all, it takes little more than a computer, e-mail, fax machine, and a phone. Is it any surprise, then, that the likes of Staples and Office Max have grown so dramatically? It also serves as an attractive alternative in luring individuals to the workplace when shortages of qualified employees occur.
- Increasingly, homes are looking more like offices and offices like homes. Or the supermarket. Or the bank. Progressive employers will sponsor services, ranging from day care (or during night shifts, on-site baby-sitting) to dry cleaners. On-line shopping will allow you to have your groceries delivered to your office or home. On-site ATM's will reside next to the candy machine. Such services are needed to accommodate the extended hours created by the employees' demand for flexible hours or from customers halfway around the globe that expect a videoconference meeting at 3 a.m.

- Another manifestation of a leaner approach to business activity will be fewer work areas. Hence, smaller facilities. The likely increase in workspace will be in conference rooms, as the workplace will be used for frequent group interactions.
- Information technology will be the singular item that forever alters the nature of work. The speed with which information can be accessed will be exponential. The world's knowledge base is now doubling in a period of less than two years, putting untold resources at one's disposal. Access to the latest in technology will create distinctions between those that can and those that can't.
- A global information network will require an increase in cultural sensitivity. At the same time, a degree of homogenization will occur through the utilization of common technical applications and a reliance on a common business language, otherwise known as English. Unfortunately, many historical distinctions and traditions will be sacrificed and lost as a result.
- Compensation disparities will escalate between the computer literate and those that aren't. Those individuals who can both learn and apply technology will be in demand and will command higher pay rates.
- For those people that wanted to use their hands in their career, brains, not brawn, will be the ticket. As noted in Workforce 2020 published by the Hudson Institute, "manufacturing's share of total U.S. employment will continue to decline due to the effects of automation and globalization. But, the millions of high-productivity manufacturing jobs that remain will be more highly skilled and better paid than anytime in U.S. history." Those that are classified as "highly skilled" will be so due to their knowledge and application of technology. Furthermore, these jobs will be safer and more stimulating.

- The concept of "career development" will shift from the traditional up-the-ladder pattern to a mode whereby an employee will operate in multiple settings and on different teams.
- The volatility of markets, speed to market, and technology will be more conducive to small and medium-sized organizations. As a consequence, significant job growth and opportunities will be evident in these smaller, emerging companies. Highly layered, bureaucratic, and heavily unionized organizations may be left in the dust of those enterprising and streamlined organizations whose eyes are on the customer and not themselves.
- In the 80's, sociologist and author, John Naisbett, coined our future society as being both "high tech" and "high touch." Since then, many persons contend there's been more "tech" and less "touch." With potential alienation and declining interpersonal skills as a consequence of an increasing technologically oriented community, virtual corporations may create such positions, believe it or not, as a "Director of Socialization" to help foster ways for more effective human interaction.
- In connection with a high value on "personal time," organizations may revisit the need for offering sabbaticals, particularly in high-stress positions. Sabbaticals not only provide opportunities to unwind, but also serve as venues for focused learning.

Any volunteers? These items are only a sample of what's ahead. Such heretofore monuments of American enterprise as the Sears Towers or Empire State Building may soon become mere symbols of a bygone era than effective work environments. Today's icons of the workplace will likely include a home office, a cell phone, a personal web page, and a *dot com* to the name of each organization. Maybe, each person. Only one's imagination can speculate on the changing landscape for the work environment of this new century.

In a similar way, we might imagine what skills and traits are necessary for our kids as the workplace transforms itself. Our kids probably already know. If you'd like to find out, read on.

Portrait of the New Worker

Radical changes. Rapid changes. As the world changes in quantum ways, so are organizations. Yet, organizations are little more than the sum of its parts, its people. Survival in an increasingly challenging and competitive environment will require the face of the *emerging worker*—a worker who bears little similarity to the worker of the 20th century.

In many ways, the transformation will be similar to a century ago when nearly 85% of the American workforce was affiliated with agriculture. Henry Ford and his cohorts inaugurated the Industrial era, compelling people to leave the farm for the factory. A person's work schedule was no longer dictated by the seasons but by thc sound of the plant's steam whistle, announcing a change of shifts. The success of a person's career was marked by how many years they endured with one organization. Most careers required little more than an 8th grade education, and men did the work. Decisions about what to do and when were strictly in the purview of a few supervisors. Rank-and-file employees amounted to little more than worker bees.

That was then.

The emerging employee of the Information Age has a whole different look. Not only is the complexion of the workplace drastically different, but the requisite attributes of the employee in the 21st century are equally so.

While the following profile is not a prescription for success, it just might be for one's survival. At least, in the employment sense. The radical changes in the workplace suggest an environment of flux, excitement, and fast pace. It will be similar to the characterization from a quote that I jotted down from an unknown author a few years ago. If you've ever done any whitewater rafting, you'll appreciate it: *We're in permanent whitewater. If you can't cope with that, get on dry land because we're on our way.*

Here are some characteristics of the emerging worker who is anxious to put his or her oars in the river:

- *Fast and flexible.* As organizations change at the flick of a switch, they'll want employees who can adapt and be resilient. Short-term assignments and project work will be common. Duties will be constantly realigned. If a person doesn't stay light on his or her feet, someone else will be waiting in the wings.
- *Versatile expertise.* While this sounds like an oxymoron, the emerging worker must demonstrate considerable expertise at creating value. But, he or she can't stay pigeon-holed. Adding skills to one's tool kit must be a constant. It's refreshing to know that this concept isn't new. Thomas Jefferson proved his versatility by being an inventor, statesman, horticulturist, architect, author, and president.
- *Perpetual learning.* With knowledge doubling every two years and changes in technology occurring even quicker, it won't take long for someone to become obsolete. Therefore, your kids will constantly be taking courses, attending seminars, reading, and pursuing appropriate certifications. As a parent, you might think about doing these things, too. Like now.
- *Think & Do.* Magazine editor, Virginia Postrel, wrote in a 1998 *Wall Street Journal* editorial, "Gone are the days of Frederick W. Taylor's (early 20th century industrialist) decree, 'You are not supposed to think. There are other people paid for thinking around here.' Nowadays, pretty much everyone gets paid for thinking." For the emerging worker, *thinking* will be synonymous with imagining new solutions, identifying areas of waste, and adding value. *Executing* those thoughts and ideas, even if they fail, is the other side of the equation. Kids are great at doing this.

- *Self-Direction.* Within the first hour of the first session of the class I teach on *Career Management & Human Development,* I begin with this premise: career management is no one's responsibility but one's *own.* Certainly, the restructuring and layoffs of the early 90's taught us that. That same premise will hold true for one-and-all in the new workplace. What one wants to do, when, and how in one's career will reside with oneself combined with some inspiration from the good Lord. Selecting and managing one's particular benefits and retirement program will also be left up to each person.
- *Behave like an Owner.* Increasingly, organizations will be an assemblage of mini-enterprises that operate independently. Employees will have unlimited access to information, insights into customer expectations, and ample authority to do something. In other words, they'll have loads of *freedom* and *responsibility.* Employees of the future will also share something else that's synonymous with business owners and entrepreneurs, specifically the thrill of the hunt. They'll be opportunists, constantly selling something they know better than anyone else: themselves. More precisely, they'll have to market their particular competencies and their special formula for making a difference.
- *Resourcefulness.* Although the computer will allow anyone to have the world at their fingertips, knowing where to go and whom to contact will be the key. In this regard, no one does it better than Harvey McKay, author of *Swim with the Sharks.* He underscores the importance of contacts by asking his audiences to name the most important work-related word in the English language. Most people respond with *hard work, creativity, strategy, selling,* or *teamwork.* His answer? The *Rolodex.*
- *Business-savvy.* In an effort at self-management and justifying one's contribution, the new worker will wear multiple hats: Human Resources Director, Chief Financial Officer, Chief Information

Officer, Buyer, and Administrative Assistant. Developing a measure of business literacy (yeah, things like understanding income statements and balance sheets) will be necessary. Thankfully, this doesn't mean everyone needs to become a CPA (who would want to live in a world of nothing but bean counters any way!).

- *Techno-smart.* What a difference ten years can make. When I was in college in the early 70's, there was a single solitary computer on campus. Yeah, just one. And it was the size of a Mack truck. Only the computer science profs and a few geeks had access to it. Less than a decade later, that monolith transformed itself, ala Bill Gates, into the PC. Gone were the typewriter, the standard Texas Instruments calculator, and that gargantuan-size campus computer. In were the Apples and the Gateways. Games, word processing, Power Point presentations, the Internet—it was all there! Now, it's only a fraction of the size and tons faster. GPS (Global Positioning Systems) are becoming standard in cars. PLC's (Programmable Logic Controls) are on nearly every piece of manufacturing equipment. Virtual Reality games have replaced the neighborhood baseball diamond. A person's ability to learn and apply technology will become a standard for academic achievement and an expectation of job performance.
- *Think Global, Speak Global.* If there ever was a time to think the world is getting smaller, now's the time. And it will only escalate—big time. Suddenly, your "neighbor" isn't the supplier down the street, but the vendor in China. Or, South Africa. Or, Brazil. We Americans haven't been accustomed to thinking beyond our borders. The rest of the world has operated in this fashion for eons. It's catch up time. So, if your child hasn't learned a second language by now, get them started. And here's one more challenge, why not learn one yourself?

- *Playful.* Several years ago, actor Tom Hanks played a big-kid role in the movie, *Big.* It was about kid who was transformed into an adult's body and was granted his wish-among-wishes: an opportunity to design all kinds of games and contraptions for a toy company. Unlike his peers, he saw things through the eye of a child. For him, *work* was *play*. The two activities were indistinguishable. That perspective made him the most valued employee in his company. OK, it's only a movie. Yet, the emerging worker will approach his daily activity less as a daily grind and more like a noontime recess. Work will require more creativity, spontaneity, responsiveness, and hastily assembled teams. Like a quick game of touch football. That type of playfulness will spur new ideas and keep better employees motivated.
- *Meekness*—Where did this word come from? What does it mean? Is it even a word? For those of us who have even a hint of its meaning, it seems so contrary to contemporary thinking. Meekness has to do with things like humility and dependence, the very opposites for "making it" in school, on the playing field, or in the workplace. Yet, *meekness* may be the most important quality because it puts things, like us, in perspective. It acknowledges that our formula for fulfillment begins with a humble acknowledgment that everything begins and ends with *grace*. God's grace. Without meekness, a person often approaches work and co-workers with some degree of presumption. With it, we allow God to shape us and our kids into the persons we're meant to be. And isn't that the bottom-line?

Work trends. Workplace changes. Workplace qualities. What remains? How about a glimpse into one more crystal ball? It's the one that speculates about jobs of the future.

Jobs in the Future

I'll never forget it. It was Christmas season in the early 80's and the most important "person" to come on the scene was no more than 24 inches tall, kind of pudgy, but with a smile that melted any young girl. Perhaps, you remember her: the original Cabbage Patch doll.

The retail price was $29.95 but, due to demand, some eager-to-please parents would pay five times as much. Once, in a suburban New York department store, some fisticuffs broke out between a set of adults who voraciously grabbed at a couple of Cabbage Patch Kids that remained on the shelf. Can't you just hear them yelling,

"Hey, I was here first!"

"No, I was here first!"

"Oh, no you weren't!"

"Oh, yes I was!"

I guess "kids" will be kids. However, whether it's Cabbage Patch dolls, the coolest car, the latest fashion, or the hottest computer software, Americans are motivated by what's HOT. We want it now! And, we'll do whatever it takes to get it! In a similar vein, many of us plan our careers by speculating on the latest and greatest. And, many do so regardless of our skills or orientation.

In my career counseling, I once encountered a young man who, even though he was a college graduate, was still totally undecided about his career direction. Between our sessions, however, he came upon a magazine article that indicated the phenomenal growth potential for computer programmers. Well, that clinched it. He arrived at our next session with a proclamation that he found his life's work: he'd become a computer programmer. Knowing some things about his personal orientation through our sessions, I silently expressed some reservations. I asked if he'd be willing to complete our discussions and assessments, if for no other reason than to verify his choice. He said OK.

We discovered that his orientation, skills, and passion were really with kids. He appeared to have all the tools to be a fantastic elementary education teacher. It would also give him the opportunity to coach some sports that he was eager to do. He weighed both options and through an honest evaluation of himself and some prayerful consideration, he elected teaching. He's still teaching and has the same level of gusto for teaching now as he did nearly 20 years ago.

This illustration is meant as a framework for a discussion about the lure of hot careers. Anyone should hesitate about selecting a career track *solely* on the basis of an article in *Time* or a two-minute clip on the nightly news about *Really Cool Jobs in the New Millennium.* I keep hearing those words of wisdom from the old bard, William Shakespeare, "This above all, to thine own self be true."

At the same time, some thoughtful exploration of career trends is equally prudent. Not surprisingly, certain fields hold more promise than others. Lots more. Those careers that do offer greater likelihood of employment, an opportunity to apply one's training or education, and greater income potential.

We've all heard stories about philosophy majors who are cab drivers or English majors who are waiting on tables because job prospects in their chosen fields were few and far between. By saying this, I'm not suggesting that the #1 factor in choosing one's vocation should be prospects for employment. Nor, am I wanting to deter someone from their *true* interests or to diminish the value of any vocation. Yet, it should compel those individuals and their educational institutions to consider some creative ways to leverage or adapt their training and their passions.

Fortunately, there are considerable resources that offer some well-reasoned speculation about the employability of various careers. Among the list of such resources, the most prominent is the *Bureau of Labor Statistics.* We've mentioned them before. They track trends upon trends. Their staff is comprised of statistical geeks who get turned on collecting data, slicing and dicing it, and publishing their findings for our benefit. Thank goodness for them.

Approximately, every two years, they render their employment projections based upon an analysis of some critically important indices, including:

- Population and labor force growth
- Percent of labor force by race (both existing and projected)
- Percent of labor force by age group
- Total job openings due to growth and replacement needs

There's a lot more that they consider but from this data they offer projections that can serve as wise counsel. For instance, 2000 BLS data indicated that 67.9% of all jobs until 2010 would not require postsecondary education. At the same time, they speculated that occupations requiring a bachelor's degree would grow the fastest. Since the BLS supplies their reports bi-annually, I'd encourage anyone to check out their reports. They're easily found on the Internet (www.bls.gov) or, as noted before, in the *Occupational Outlook Handbook.* A school counselor or librarian should also have this information.

While projections on specific careers may vary and should be investigated by yourself or your child, the data is pointing to occupational growth in several key areas. Here's a "Top 10" of the sectors where job growth will prosper (in alphabetical order):

- Education
- Energy & Utilities
- Entertainment
- Financial Services
- Health care
- Management
- Marketing, advertising, and public relations
- Social Work

- Technology
- Telecommunications

It's no big surprise that the three biggies within this list are jobs in technology, education, and health care. Computer engineers, technicians, and systems analysts are needed almost at an exponential rate in order to develop and service the ever changing and growing applications of technology. This demand will be driven from three sectors.

In one area, technology will become *the* ticket to increases in both productivity and profitability. As noted before, it's rare today to see a manufacturing operation that hasn't integrated PLC's (programmable logic controls) that monitor a machine's various functions. New computer-monitored distribution methods will also regulate the ebb-and-flow of products between suppliers, the organization, and the customer. At any given moment, anyone in the food chain will be able to check the status of an order.

Technology is also driving perhaps the most exciting phenomenon of our generation: the Internet and E-commerce. B2B (business-to-business) applications are being facilitated through the Internet. Individuals are utilizing the Internet not only for communication and entertainment, but also for ordering products. A friend of mine orders her weekly groceries off the Internet and has them delivered to her home. Being the penny-pinching type (I can relate!), she only opted for this only if the prices were less—and they were by 10%.

To provide all the transmissions and communications that we'll require, a burgeoning area of technology will be in telecommunications. I won't get technical with you, but an increasing need for bandwidth is quickly becoming a necessity since it offers more capacity for multiple transmissions: telephones, cable television, Internet, etc. In addition, an integration of voice, video, and data will foster a whole new demand for research technicians and installation specialists. If only Alexander Graham Bell could see us now.

The next growing job sector will be in education. We've discussed the simple fact that learning will be a race with no finish line, an event without a conclusion. The learning process will be an extended school year for kids and a standard performance requirement for adults. Educators will be needed more for development and less for instruction since the delivery systems will occur more often through one's PC. Web-based training will make learning convenient and cost effective. Furthermore, the preponderance of knowledge, new software, and changing skill sets will compel every worker to learn, learn, and learn some more. If not, there's someone else in the world—literally—who's waiting in the batter's box for an opportunity to perform.

The third significant arena is health care. And, it's no surprise. After all, we Baby Boomers won't be babies forever. Many of us try, however. And we're willing to do whatever it takes, courtesy of pharmaceuticals, surgical procedures, and fitness programs, to extend ourselves. To court this desire, more will be invested in research and development, particularly in the pharmaceutical industry. Biotechnology and gene therapy will explore ways to alter life for both young and old. Also, new advances in medical devices may bear evidence that the "bionic man" (or woman) is more fact than fiction in the not-too-distant future. If the average age of an American jumped from 47 years of age in 1900 to 76 in 2000, who's willing to wager that the average life span in 2100 cold be 95? Do I hear 105? 110?

Getting us there will be a collection of health care specialists beyond the research scientist. Nutritionists, home health care aids, and insurance claims processors are all part of the team. Exercise equipment manufacturers and personal trainers will become increasingly popular. Assisted-living centers will offer ample opportunities as these new neighborhoods blend health care, accommodations, social interaction, and adult supervision. Nicely, the health care industry won't mandate an RN or a MD degree; most opportunities will require a certificate or an Associates degree.

Plotting a strategy with an eye toward job growth by various sectors makes sense—in many ways, good *business* sense. It's not a one-time event, however. The volatility of the market place, global competitiveness, and new changes in technology will vary the degree of new and attractive opportunities.

Keeping one eye on the future and the other one on one's current performance will pay dividends. It also reinforces the concept of "versatile expertise" that was noted in the earlier section. The emerging worker must constantly demonstrate a high level of expertise without staying pigeonholed. Focusing on the trends, the opportunities that are likely to occur in the future, and the skills that are necessary to capture those opportunities will the ticket for the wild ride ahead for your kids.

What else with that ride be like? Only time will tell. But, as things change, we need to ask ourselves one more fundamental question, and it's this: is there a *purpose* to this ride we call a "career?" And if so, what is it? Let's think about this in the next and final chapter.

Chapter IX

The Value of "Vocation"

It's another Monday morning at my house. My pre-work ritual begins at 6 a.m. with my radio alarm. The "morning personality" of a local radio station jerks and jolts all his listeners with the wakening words, "Time to get up-up-up, and head out for another day in the salt pits!" It's his daily headliner. Wow, do I ever get fired up for the day with those words of encouragement!

After shaving, dressing, having my devotions, and a quick bowl of cereal, I'm off to my favorite coffee shop, J.P.'s, for a quick cup of dark roast. Mondays always have an extra measure of customers, as more caffeine is required to get the workweek going.

Next, I'm off for the 1.4 mile route to work that includes a mere two traffic signals (yes, I do count my blessings for those of you who must daily endure 58,000 of them). Occasionally, I stop at a light behind a certain commuter going my same way. I know him by his bumper sticker. It reads, "My worst day fishing is better than my best day at work." And then, as I'm pulling into the parking lot at work, I hear one more commercial. This one is from the restaurant, *T.G.I. Friday's*. By their very name, they're already talking about Friday, and it's only Monday!

Maybe, it's just a coincidence, but am I sensing a theme here?

Increasingly, it seems we endure an existence that lives for weekends, the 5 o'clock hour, a coveted fourth week of vacation, or early retirement. In other words, anything but "work."

Somehow, the word has acquired anything but a positive reputation. Studs Terkel in his famed book, *Working,* paraphrased one of his subjects who characterized work as "a Monday through Friday sort of dying." Although most of us might not describe our jobs in such a macabre fashion, we probably view it as a $$ means to an end, and not as something with *real* meaning.

If so, maybe it's time to reevaluate "work" for what it is, for what it is intended to be, and definitely what it should be for our kids. I contend there are three primary ways to examine work. One way has to do with viewing "work" as "vocation." In this chapter, we'll briefly examine work and occupations in the context of the original meaning of vocation, namely, one's particular "calling" and how that plays out in all the hats we wear. A second way is considering it from the perspective of our personal integrity—whether we're being true to our real selves. And thirdly, we'll think about "work" as "Kingdom stuff," looking at what we do and what your kids will do as having a bigger-than-life impact.

Sound pretty heavy? We'll keep it light. Sound important? You bet. Basically, if we don't rethink our perception of "work," we only transmit the message one more time as well as to one more generation, namely to your kids and my kids.

Here's another way of looking at it. One time, a person saw three workers at a construction site. He asked them what they were doing. The first man said, "I'm breaking rocks." The second said, "I'm earning a living." The third answered, "I'm helping to build a cathedral."

It all comes down to this: Do you want your kids to be splitting rocks or building magnificent cathedrals?

Work as "Vocation"

For 28 years, my grandfather worked in a shoe factory. The factory was 2 1/2 blocks from his bungalow-type house. For all those years, he walked past 19 similar-type homes en route to a two-story non-descript brick factory where he stitched shoe upon shoe upon shoe upon shoe. It wasn't until after his death that I learned a few more details about his life as a cobbler, including the tough, militaristic atmosphere that characterized his plant.

I doubt that I knew little about his work-life because he disguised it. A Theory X management approach wasn't his style and, fortunately, he never became a practitioner, particularly when it came to his family. While I vaguely knew him as a shoe-maker, I came to appreciate him as so much more: a consummate story-teller, a fisherman, a practical joker, a Boy Scout troop leader, a church deacon, and the neighborhood repairman. Above all, he was a dedicated Christian who saw his life as more than the sum of his parts or his roles. For Grandpa, his various "occupations" were secondary to his "vocation."

Although I strongly suspect my grandfather never studied Latin, he must have known intuitively the Latin derivative of "vocation" which is "vocare." It means, "to call." I think he knew that his *real* calling—his vocation—was to be a servant. He wove his servant-attitude into every activity and every hat he wore.

Ben Patterson, chaplain at Hope College and author of *The Grand Essentials,* relates a similar story. "When John Wanamaker was Postmaster General of the United States, he was very involved in overseeing the Sunday school of his church. He was asked, "How do you get the time to run the post office and the Sunday school, too?"

He answered, "Why, the Sunday school is my business! All other things are just things. Forty-five years ago, I decided that God's promise was sure: 'Seek first the Kingdom of God, and his righteousness, and all these things will be added unto you.'" As Patterson offers, "There was a man who had his vocation in charge of his occupation, not the reverse."

This business about our true vocation doesn't come easy. Think about it for a moment. When was the last time you struck up a conversation with someone, exchanged greetings, asked the mandatory question, "And what do you do?" and heard a response, "I'm a servant." Or, "an encourager." Or, "a steward."

Not lately, I'm sure.

As adults, we tend to be title chasers. We admire those who possess the label of "Vice-President" or "Director" or "Doctor." In our haste to achieve such status, we become one-with-our-job. Sometimes, we over-identify ourselves with our jobs. Such a characterization is especially evident when a person is laid-off or terminated. Job loss becomes loss of self. And, it's not limited to working adults or professionals. Can you recall my experience with my freshman classmates in college? I observed similar symptoms when a pre-med classmate failed Organic Chemistry. Their hopes of medical school and eventually, a medical career were dashed.

When we experience this or create expectations of this type for others, we've misdirected and rewritten the true meaning of "vocation." Dr. Paul Powers in *Love Your Job* reminds us that "It's one thing to love your job and revel in doing it every day. It's another to lose yourself completely in that job, or to let that job completely define you. Identify *with* your job, but don't identify yourself *as* that job." Words of wisdom. When we identify *with* a job, an interest, or our studies we do so because our gifts are acting out. Our "calling" is speaking our language in ways that work. We've then begun to realize our true vocation and our personhood.

Like most things, such revelations don't come quickly. We may have to take the scenic route to understand, let alone appreciate, the significance of our vocation. One such pilgrim is Mary Richards who shares her personal journey in *Centering on Pottery, Poetry, and the Person.* She shares, "It seemed strange to me, as to others, that, having taken my Ph.D. in English, I should then in the middle of my life, instead of taking up a college professorship, turn to the art of pottery. During one period, when people asked me what I did, I was uncertain what to answer; I guessed I could say I taught English, wrote poetry, and made pottery. What was my occupation? I finally gave up and said 'Person.'"

Therefore, ponder a couple of questions for you on behalf of your kids.

- What "vocation" are you sensing within your son or your daughter?

- How easy or difficult will it be for you to minimize a focus on a specific job "title" for your child versus discerning and articulating their "vocation?"
- What might you do to further prompt that real vocation within your child?

Vocation and Integrity

Time for a trivia question: what male vocalist earned his fourth Grammy award for his *MTV Unplugged* special in 1995? Here's a hint: He received the award at the tender age of 69. And he's had more appearances on *The David Letterman Show* than any other male singer. It's none other than the famed balladeer, Tony Bennett. His smooth, crooning style is alluring to all as evidenced by his familiarity to both my parent's generation and the MTV crowd. While he is also gaining fame as a painter, his long-standing talent is singing. On this note, he offers, "singing is not a choice. I have to sing. It's not my ambition. I just have to. I have to sing and paint. That's what I do, and that's what I love to do."

Have to. Love to. I think those sentiments resonate with another, somewhat earlier, master, William Shakespeare who penned,

This above all: to thine own self be true,
And it must follow, as the night the day,
Thou can not then be false to any man.

For Bennett, Shakespeare, and others, anything outside of being "true to self" is dishonest, if not deceitful. It lacks *integrity.* And if there's any place for integrity, it must be at the core of our vocational calling.

Incorporating integrity in our career begins with that fundamental recognition of our "anchors" (Dr. Edgar Schein) which are those gifts, skills, traits, and preferences that mark each of us. It's what we described earlier as one's *imprint.* It's an honest acceptance of our gifts and an innate desire to put them to use.

I once encountered an absence of this type of integrity in Chad, a high-spirited young man in his early twenties. I met him at a time when he was working on a production line for a furniture company. He was torn about a career direction for his young life, but was enticed by what he heard and saw in a newspaper article, entitled, "Jobs of the Future." All the top careers pointed to a common item: computers. He thought it would be neat to become a computer programmer, since the employment prospects were unlimited. After a few conversations with him, however, it was crystal clear this guy was anything but analytical. His anchors were rock solid in people, particularly kids. He enjoyed mentoring them, coaching them, interacting with them. We pursued this in some detail with sage advice from William Shakespeare, the apostle Paul, and a bunch of others about being true to ourselves. Today, this young man is a middle-ager who has just finished his 14th year teaching physical education in an elementary school. And his love for kids is just as fresh today as it was more than 14 years ago. That's cool. That's integrity.

As this story suggests, being true to ourselves has the potential of delivering good news and bad news. It certainly offers opportunities but it equally, if not more, poses limitations. It may mean sacrifice. You see, if I really am honest about my *imprint*, I'll focus primarily on my particular gifts and not others, no matter how attractive and lucrative they appear.

Ouch!

Suddenly, the smorgasbord of things to do, skills to develop, and opportunities to pursue might just have to be scaled down. That hurts. And it almost sounds un-American. Ours has become a society that wants us to *see* all, *do* all, and *be* all. While that sounds mighty tempting, we flirt with much and commit to little. We bounce from option to option, never fully developing our anchors in a way that produces in-depth satisfaction.

Being honest to oneself can also play havoc with one other issue: the cunning need for status. We pay homage to it in any possible way: from type of automobile to brand of blue jeans. From Rolex watches to water front property. It's equally evident in the workplace: white collar vs. blue collar; professional vs. laborer, college bound vs. non-college bound. As our society has created such dichotomies, we've also cast a certain level of prestige, deference to, and envy of specific job titles—titles like CEO, Executive Director, Superintendent, Senior Administrator, or Doctor. We're encouraged, cajoled, or prodded to diligently pursue any career that typically offers a high level of renown and an even higher amount of income.

While there's not anything inherently wrong in urging each other and especially our kids to "go for the gold," there's more to be said in prompting them to "be the best they can be."

Being the best they can be begins with being the best with what they have been given. That's integrity. It's appropriately characterized in a Jewish Hasidic tale about an early Jewish rabbi by the name of Rabbi Zusya. When he was an old man, he said, "In the coming world, they will not ask me: 'Why were you not Moses?' They will ask me: 'Why were you not Zusya?'

The product of personal integrity, of being true to ourselves, yields a couple of attractive benefits. Here's the first one: *fun*! A couple of testimonies speak to it:

> *To love what you do and feel that it matters—how could anything be more fun?*
>
> Katherine Graham
> former editor of *The Washington Post*

> *The master in the art of living makes little distinction between his work and his play, his labor and his leisure. He hardly knows which is which. He simply pursues his vision of excellence at whatever he does, leaving others to decide whether he is working or playing. To him, he's always doing both!*
>
> James Michener
> author

I can't believe I'm actually getting paid to do this job!
Johnny Carson
former host of *The Tonight Show*

OK, let's temper things a little bit. Our work and our careers are not going to be fun-and-games 24 hours a day. I'm sure Jerry Seinfeld or Michael Jordan have had their down days. Yet, those who take pleasure from their work are usually honest about one other thing: they recognize their place in their work. Sensing one's role in the theater of other people and their gifts is viewed as another benefit. I'll try to explain courtesy of an event that happens only once every four years: the Olympics.

In my opinion, the Olympics are one of the world's most spectacular events. The thrill of victory, the agony of defeat, nations' flags and national anthems, and awesome opening and closing ceremonies—all of these make this once-every-four-years event truly special. For the extent of two weeks, the TV is my constant companion. Believe it or not, the climatic moment of the Olympics for me is not a particular competition but the final ten minutes on the very last day. The commentators have finished their remarks and all that remains is a visual and musical montage of the best performances.

Something else is happening simultaneously, however, during those last ten minutes: the credits. And it's not just the producer and director. Literally, hundreds of names roll before your eyes. They're persons who for at least the previous four years have been associated with the TV production of this most major of sporting events. It's a Herculean effort that required the efforts of persons from a third tier technician to a copy writer, from a host's make-up artist to a team of multi-lingual translators. Somehow, the network doesn't do justice to its own squad of players by passing through those names at 60 mph, but at least there's a mini-second for each person.

The whole production comes together because of the collective efforts of each person's talent. The exercise of complementary—not competitive—skills and talents makes the production happen. It's the application of each person's particular contribution, ala their *imprint*, and those of everybody else that makes a TV image materialize, a manufacturing company work, a school system flourish, and a family function successfully.

Greater minds than mine recognized this a long time ago. The apostle Paul illustrated this fact when comparing the makeup of a church with the parts of a body. In 1 Corinthians 12, he says, "Now the body is not made up on one part, but of many. If the foot should say, 'Because I am not a hand, I do not belong to the body,' it would not cease to be part of the body. In fact, God has arranged the parts in the body, every one of them, just as he wanted them to be. If they were all one part, where would the body be? As it is, there are many parts, but one body."

Witnessing a synchronous organization really hum is something beautiful. Those who participate in it usually relish the collective result while subtly knowing their role in making it happen. It's a benefit that goes beyond self. And the results are usually pretty spectacular. Maybe even eternal. Our next and final section will speak to that aspect.

Kingdom Work

Most of us are familiar with the "Nobel Prize" and may even know something about the man whose namesake this award honors. Yet, it highly doubtful this prize would ever have happened if it hadn't been for a misprint in a local paper.

Alfred Nobel began his day like most of us with breakfast, a cup of coffee, and the newspaper. Upon glancing through the paper, he came upon the obituaries and noticed the name of someone he was quite familiar with: himself! If that doesn't wake you up in the morning, nothing will! It appears the paper had mistakenly printed the obituary notice of him versus his brother who had died a couple of days earlier. The article accurately acknowledged him as the inventor of dynamite and as the man who made a fortune selling explosives to governments worldwide. While he was justifiably appalled to read about his premature death, he was even more shocked and disturbed to think that he would be remembered as the merchant of death and destruction. It prompted him to rethink himself and his ultimate legacy. At that moment, he decided to transform his fame and fortune into a foundation that distributed awards to those whose accomplishments had benefited humanity. He intentionally departed from that which had made him successful, aiming the next part of his life in another direction.

"Another direction." Sometimes, it takes a big-time life experience, such as Nobel's, to contemplate what Life is all about and to move the compass 180 degrees. Sometimes, that "big event" is the day we retire. Until that day, most adults believe they have to earn their dues, accumulate a certain number of "things," and have a sweet nest egg in their 401(k) before beginning to think about the deeper things of life. In his successful book, *Half Time,* Bob Buford believes that adults can point to a more meaningful direction at a somewhat earlier stage, specifically the *second* half of life. He contends that a second half game plan can move an individual from "success to significance." As a result, the second half can be much better than the first.

I respectfully disagree. While there is much to Buford's ideas and strategy, "significance" doesn't need a time line. Significance can present itself at <u>any</u> age.

In the first chapter of this book, I used an illustration from the provocative movie, *The Dead Poet's Society.* Unlike his fellow instructors who were solely accountable for getting their graduates into prestigious universities, teacher John Keating challenged his students with the admonition, *carpe diem* (seize the day). More precisely, he dared them to seize *this* day. His contention was that a person didn't have to wait and become an accomplished patent attorney, physician, or senior vice-president to experience significance. As the movie concluded, several of his students assumed the challenge. And while the movie doesn't indicate whatever happened to those students, it's fairly good odds that those young men made a difference and realized genuine significance *both* as they journeyed through school and into their careers. It's something your children can realize, too. Even now.

But "significance" for what? Let's sum it up as "things for the Kingdom"—as in the "heavenly" type. It's the realization and acceptance that there's a Kingdom that compels our present calling and awaits our eventual conclusion. It represents a better future but also a current reality where God's purposes can be evidenced and realized. And it definitely has truly vital implications when it comes to our vocational calling.

Career Profile: ***Paul Hillegonds, Speaker of the House, Michigan House of Representatives***

My parents did not try to steer me toward a particular career. They emphasized that I had responsibility to work hard and use my God-given abilities.

From my father, I gained an appreciation of history and the need to care about and be engaged in what is going on in the community and our world. Through him, I learned to value public service and the pursuit of ideals. He stressed the importance of setting goals and being open to life's opportunities.

My mother, by example, encouraged me to achieve balance in life between one's professional ambitions, spiritual health, and family. From her inner peace, I have come to appreciate that each of life's milestones has a purpose and that one's professional future will take care of itself if you labor with love and faith.

In his book, *Serving God,* Ben Patterson shares, "One good way to figure out what that (our vocation) might be is on the basis of how our God-given talents and gifts match up with what God wants done in the world. Frederick Buechner's whimsical definition of vocation is just that: 'The place God calls you to is the place where your deep gladness and the world's deep hunger meet.'"

Bill Hillegonds, my college chaplain in the 70's, explained it in a similar way. He characterized the world as a large "ball of need." He elaborated by suggesting, "What you have to do is prepare yourself and then focus on a specific area of need. Next, transform it into God's kingdom—or at least move it, nudge it, toward God's kingdom." Who would ever have thought that a ball of need could be transfigured into things for the Kingdom? Yet, isn't that what we want our lives and our career to be about?

I've tried to tap into this question with both my clients and my graduate students. Whether I'm counseling or teaching, I furnish an assignment which asks them to compose a written response to this question: "How, if at all, do you want the world to be positively impacted by what you do in your career?" After a week or so, I often get one of the following responses:

- I'm sorry, but I didn't write anything. This was too hard!
- I really don't care if what I do makes a difference or not.
- I'll make more of a difference in how I raise my kids.
- I prefer to do something worthwhile in my outside, volunteer activities—not my job.

Although not my students, others have offered something different. Like this one from perhaps, the least likely of vocations: a poultry farmer:

I guess it's kind of genetic. My great grandpa was a farmer, but his real interest was in raising chickens. My grandpa picked up on that and became a full-time chicken-and-egg farmer and my dad who tripled the size of our farm followed him. And now, it's my turn.

Two years ago, something happened that changed my whole attitude about raising chickens. It was the spring of the year when lots of bad storms hit the South and Midwest. I'll never forget it. It was on a Thursday night and we were watching the news right before bed. The lead story was about a tornado that destroyed a town in Arkansas. I mean, it whiped out the whole place. They interviewed a farmer whose whole chicken farm was taken out. Over 2,000 birds. This poor man's livelihood was gone in seconds.

Well, that man's work was also my own. Even though we were hundreds of miles apart, we had a common job. And because of that, I felt I had to give some of my own to get him re-started. By calling the Chamber of Commerce in that town in Arkansas, I was able to get the name of guy. With the help of a few of my neighbors, I loaded a semi with 1500 birds, plenty of feed, and some cash to help him start build a new chicken coop. Two days later, we arrived, met that farmer, and delivered our stuff.

But that's not the end of the story. In church, the following Sunday, our pastor talked about the Good Shepherd and how He tended his flocks. It hit me that both the Good Shepherd and I had the same interest in farming as well as caring for flocks—no matter if they were sheep or chickens—or another farmer. That experience gave me a new sense of me.

From a farmer to a stock broker, here's another account:

No question about it—I have been blessed. After successfully working for a major brokerage firm in Chicago, I decided to fulfill a long-long dream: venturing out on my own. Sure, I approached going solo with plenty of fear and trepidation (yeah, I knew the statistics about start-up businesses). But, I also found confidence in taking on the Lord as my partner. As predicted, the first three years were tough. They stretched my family and me financially and emotionally, but we persevered. I reminded myself that if the Israelites could make it for 40 years in the wilderness, I with the Lord's help should be able to weather a fraction of what they endured.

As I said, we've been blessed. I now manage a business with 3 outstanding brokers. While we have been rewarded handsomely, this business has allowed us to do things with clients that we're even more excited about. As expected, it's created opportunities for us to plan and fulfill our client's long-term goals. Yet, the business has also given us opportunities to brainstorm with our clients some ways that they might do things with their earnings for the common good. We've seen some individuals provide resources for projects, ranging from foreign orphanages to local Big Brother/Big Sister programs. We had one client underwrite a student in her seminary training and another who contributed nicely to Habitat for Humanity. We're now hearing from clients who are more interested in learning about the status of their pet project or program and not their portfolio! It really puts things in perspective, doesn't it?

And then, one more. This one a simple statement from a simple woman:

> *I am a pencil in the hand of God, writing a love letter to the world.*
>
> Mother Theresa

In each of these situations, it's apparent that someone made an effort to reach out and touch someone. Lester DeKoster, in his book, *Work: The Meaning of Your Life,* labels work as "the form in which we make ourselves useful to others." And while there's an abundance of vocations where people are helping people, there are even more jobs that, on face value, would seem to have no connection to aiding others, let alone being something of eternal value. (I think there's a joke about attorneys here, but we'll dispense with this for the moment.) Jobs, such as a mill operator, a label maker, or baggage handler, are easy targets for this kind of analysis.

But our judgments about these and other occupations aren't new. In the book, *Jerusalem in the Time of Jesus,* Joachim Jeremias indicates that several classifications in the first century were ranked as "sinful" since they were either immoral or made the worker ceremonially unclean. Among such evil occupations was a shepherd, many of whom were known to steal without getting caught. Yet, who called himself the Good Shepherd but none other than Jesus himself? Shepherds were also the first to herald Christ's birth.

In the final analysis, our vocation calls us to be nothing less than two qualities: obedient and faithful. Not necessarily successful. As we noted earlier, that's a tough pill to swallow in a society that acknowledges status and success. Anything less seemingly doesn't count. And that's an especially tall order for parents. Yet, as Paul noted to Timothy, "We brought nothing into the world, and we can take nothing out of it." (I Tim. 6:17). As my friend Ben Patterson observes, "Our dignity does not come from what we have, but from what we have done with what has been given to us. It comes from answering God's call to be stewards of his creation." That's Kingdom stuff.

A parting thought. One of the sacraments in most churches, including our own, is baptism. While everyone is silently placing bets as to whether or not the baby will wail when it's time for the minister to hold the child, I'm fascinated when the minister asks the parents, "And what is the Christian name of this child?" Each name has a special meaning or special connection. The sacrament also evokes a memory from years ago when our former minister, prior to returning the baby to his or her parents, would offer these words: "The Lord called you by name. Therefore, make your name count for Christ." Making your name count for Christ is participating in a Kingdom plan. While what we do is ultimately a matter of personal choice, the foundation and framework for doing so certainly begins at home.

Hopefully, this book has pointed toward this. As parents, you have been encouraged to be agents in identifying and affirming your child's unique imprint and then prompting them to live out their vocation in the compelling theater and the great adventure of God's kingdom. It's a simple mandate and a daunting responsibility, but always a journey of love.

Thankfully, we don't do it solo. We're aided by the breath of God as portrayed in these words by poet Joyce Rupp:

A small wooden flute,
an empty, hollow reed,
rests in her silent hand.
It awaits the breath
of one who creates song
through its open form.
My often empty life
rests in the hand of God;

like the hollowed flute,
it yearns for the melody
which only Breath can give.
The small, wooden flute and I,
we need the one who breathes,
we await one who makes melody.
And the one whose touch creates,
awaits our empty ordinary forms,
so that the song-starved world
may be fed with golden melodies.

The world is eagerly waiting to hear your child's special tune. What a melody that promises to be.

Appendix

Appendix A

The Nine Dot Exercise (correct answer/design)

```
o  x  x x x x x o x x x x x x x o x x x x x x x x
x  x                                          x
x    x                                     x
x     x                                 x
x       x                             x
x         x                         x
x           x                    x
o             o                o
x                x          x
x                  x      x
x                    x  x
x                    x  x
x                  x     x
x                x          x
o             o                o (start here)
x           x
x         x
x       x
x     x
x   x
x x
x
```

Appendix B

Pop Quiz

Instructions: Please respond to each statement with an appropriate number per the answer key (see below). Your answers should reflect your true feelings and not necessarily those of others, society, or current trends. Whenever possible, your answers should reflect the frequency and consistency of your actions and behaviors—in other words, how you operate most of the time.

Key:
5 = extremely/90% of the time/ daily
4 = mostly/quite frequently/the majority of the time
3 = sometimes/about 50% of the time
2 = not usually/infrequent//doubtful
1 = almost never/extremely rare/less than 10% of the time/doesn't apply

Place the most appropriate number per each statement in the blank that precedes each statement.

______1. You tell your children "I love you" at least once each day.
______2. It's important to you to work for a "family friendly" organization, permitting you to occasionally attend a school event during working hours e.g. your child's school play or soccer match.
______3. Your home and neighborhood are sufficiently safe and secure.
______4. You are intentional about exposing your kids to different people, ideas, cultures, and careers.

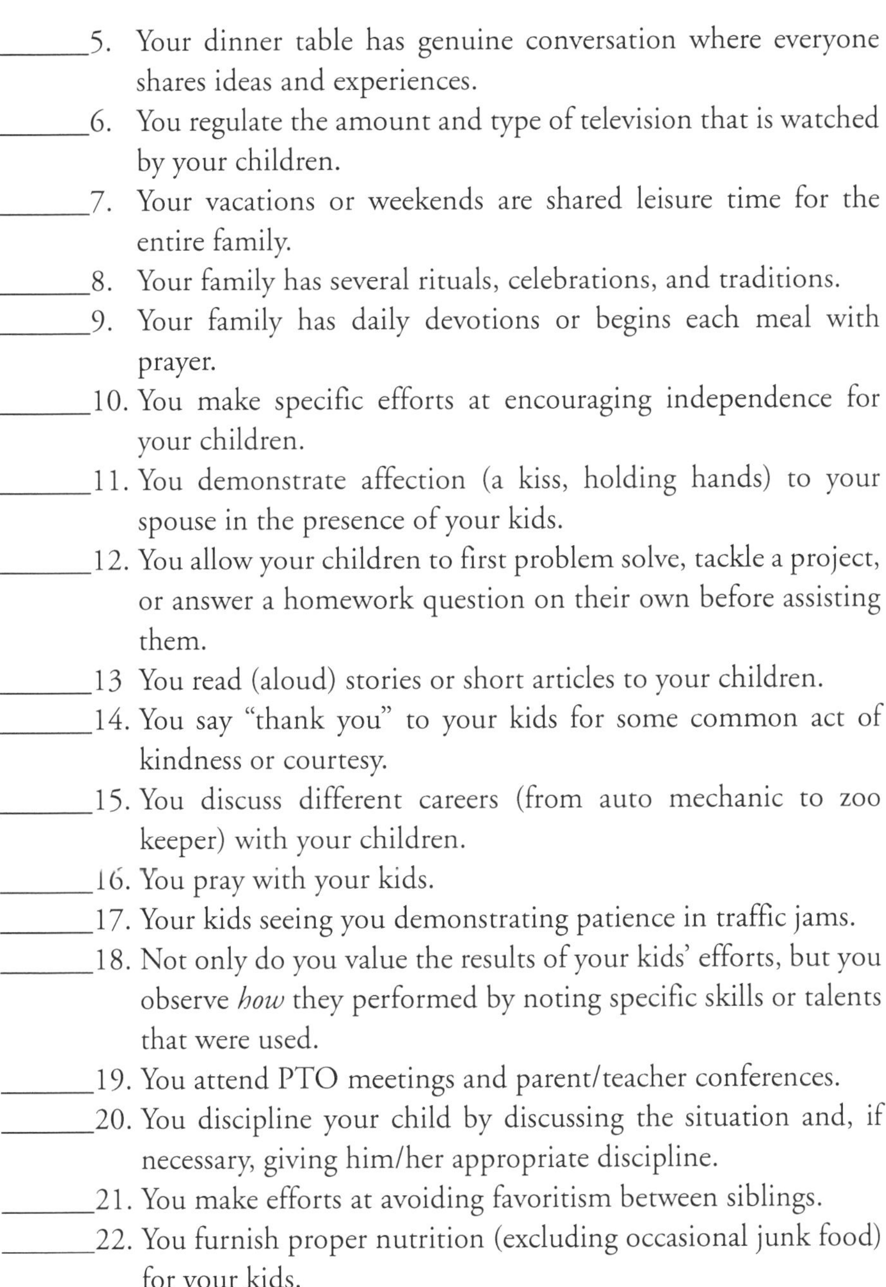

_______5. Your dinner table has genuine conversation where everyone shares ideas and experiences.

_______6. You regulate the amount and type of television that is watched by your children.

_______7. Your vacations or weekends are shared leisure time for the entire family.

_______8. Your family has several rituals, celebrations, and traditions.

_______9. Your family has daily devotions or begins each meal with prayer.

_______10. You make specific efforts at encouraging independence for your children.

_______11. You demonstrate affection (a kiss, holding hands) to your spouse in the presence of your kids.

_______12. You allow your children to first problem solve, tackle a project, or answer a homework question on their own before assisting them.

_______13 You read (aloud) stories or short articles to your children.

_______14. You say "thank you" to your kids for some common act of kindness or courtesy.

_______15. You discuss different careers (from auto mechanic to zoo keeper) with your children.

_______16. You pray with your kids.

_______17. Your kids seeing you demonstrating patience in traffic jams.

_______18. Not only do you value the results of your kids' efforts, but you observe *how* they performed by noting specific skills or talents that were used.

_______19. You attend PTO meetings and parent/teacher conferences.

_______20. You discipline your child by discussing the situation and, if necessary, giving him/her appropriate discipline.

_______21. You make efforts at avoiding favoritism between siblings.

_______22. You furnish proper nutrition (excluding occasional junk food) for your kids.

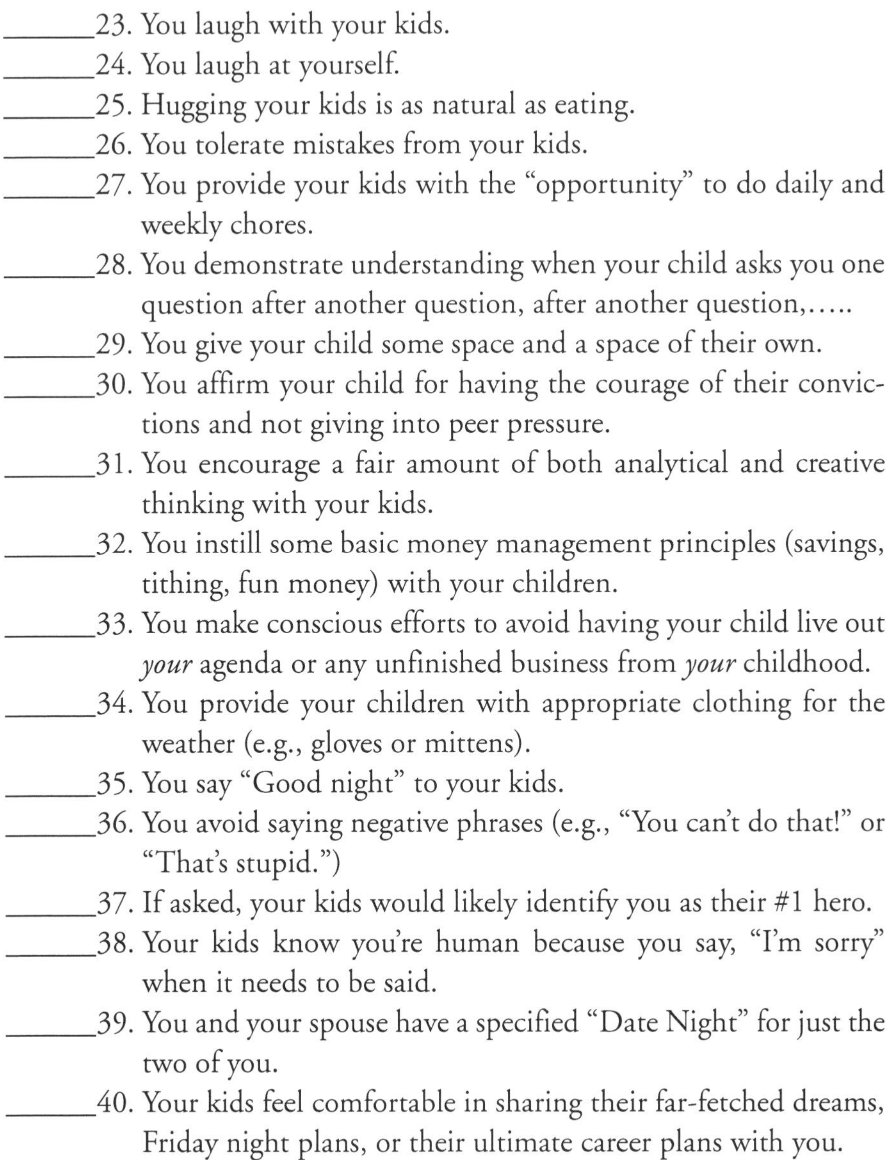

______23. You laugh with your kids.
______24. You laugh at yourself.
______25. Hugging your kids is as natural as eating.
______26. You tolerate mistakes from your kids.
______27. You provide your kids with the "opportunity" to do daily and weekly chores.
______28. You demonstrate understanding when your child asks you one question after another question, after another question,.....
______29. You give your child some space and a space of their own.
______30. You affirm your child for having the courage of their convictions and not giving into peer pressure.
______31. You encourage a fair amount of both analytical and creative thinking with your kids.
______32. You instill some basic money management principles (savings, tithing, fun money) with your children.
______33. You make conscious efforts to avoid having your child live out *your* agenda or any unfinished business from *your* childhood.
______34. You provide your children with appropriate clothing for the weather (e.g., gloves or mittens).
______35. You say "Good night" to your kids.
______36. You avoid saying negative phrases (e.g., "You can't do that!" or "That's stupid.")
______37. If asked, your kids would likely identify you as their #1 hero.
______38. Your kids know you're human because you say, "I'm sorry" when it needs to be said.
______39. You and your spouse have a specified "Date Night" for just the two of you.
______40. Your kids feel comfortable in sharing their far-fetched dreams, Friday night plans, or their ultimate career plans with you.

Appendix C

Pop Quiz Scoring Key

Instructions: Add all the numbers and place the number on the line labeled, **Your Total**. Following this, go back over the quiz and highlight those items you rated with either a 5,2, or 1.

Your Total________

Points	Rating	Description
170-200	Excellent	You must have a "SP" on your chest for "Super Parent." Patent your magic formula, then write a book about it and get on the speaking circuit.
140-169	Very good	You're practically the model parent. You take your role seriously, but you have a lot of fun with it, too. Parenthood suits you nicely.
110-139	Good	Overall, you're a good parent. For the most part, you're there for your kids, but you recognize a few areas that need some improvement (check out those items you rated as a "1" or "2").
80-109	Less than satisfactory	Parenting seems to be more work and less fun. More doses of TLC, time with the kids, and maybe a little help from your friends—or some experts—will help to turn this around.

79 or less	Needs improvement	Time for a major reality check and an even bigger mid-course correction. You probably need a new (or even a first-time) road map to help you with being an effective parent. Seek out some positive role models who can offer some helpful professional advice. Read Chapter II carefully and create some mini-action plans to help you and your kids.

Appendix D

The "Ex Files"

Key:
P = pre-kindergarten
L = lower elementary grades
U = upper elementary grades
M = middle school age
S = senior high school age
A = any age

"Ex"posure	"Ex"perience
*Surf the World Wide Web (A)	Shadow someone in the work place (M,S)
Subscribe to a magazine of the child's choice. (L, U, M, S)	Conduct an information interview at the person's workplace. (M, S)
Play the "I Saw" game in which the parent asks the child at the end of the day, "What did you see today that was special or different or something you never really saw before?" (L, U)	Volunteer in some community service project or social service function (M, S)
Window shop (P, L, U)	Participate in "Take Your Child to Work" Day (U, M)
Stop by historical markers along the road and talk about the person whom the marker commemorates (A)	Participate in Junior Achievement (S)

Take nature walks (P, L, U)

Set up a road-side stand, e.g., Lemonade stand (L, U)

Visit a Children's Museum (P, L, U)

Sell something door-to-door (U, M)

Visit a Planetarium (P, L, U, M)

Teach or tutor another child (S)

Talk to grandparents and great-grandparents about life when they were kids (A)

Participate in an apprenticeship program (S)

Read biographies (U, M, S)

Get a part-time job (S)

"Ex"posure	"Ex"perience
Check out and monitor the construction of a building project. If possible, talk to the architect, engineers, or construction manager (U, M, S)	Participate in a co-op program (S)
Become a pen pal (U, M, S)	Join a sports team in a sport of their choice (L,U,M,S)
Attend plays, concerts, operas, musical events (A)	Encourage your child to participate in extra-curricular activities (L, U, M, S)
Attend a lecture by a noted authority (M, S)	Attend Summer Camp (U, M)
Participate in hands-on creative activities that are sponsored by your community's Arts Association (P, L, U)	Attend a specialty summer camp program (S)
Enroll your son or daughter in a "leisure" type (hobby) class through your area's Community Education program (M, S)	Research, present, and participate in a Science Fair (M, S)
Visit and browse through a bookstore (A)	If your school has one, participate in a "Career Academy" which, in some cases, is a year long, in-depth exposure to various careers (S)
Purchase a camera for your child and have them take pictures of anything. Yes, anything. (L, U, M, S)	Take an "Alternative Vacation" in which your family substitutes a typical vacation for an extensive service project-type one. (M, S)

Have a foreign student from a local college over for supper (M, S)

Host a foreign student for a semester (M, S)

Purchase or borrow a telescope and check out the solar system (E, U, M, S)

Study a foreign language (A)

Visit an art gallery (U, M, S)

Accompany a police officer or a Emergency Medical Technician (EMT) for a shift (S)

Ask your child about a favorite product, store, or entertainment place. Then, buy one share of that stock and have them monitor it (M, S)

Keep a diary (U, M, S)

Serve as an intern for a governmental official or a political party (S)

"Ex"posure

Subscribe to the *Occupational Outlook Quarterly,* a publication about specific careers and job trends (S)

Check out the booths at a local convention or professional meeting (A)

Visit historical sites, particularly those that feature "living history." (L, U, M, S)

Have a meal at an authentic ethnic restaurant (M, S)

Read a good book with your child (P, L, U)

Attend "Story Time" at your local library (P, L)

Purchase an Encyclopedia and encourage your children to both browse through it and use it as a resource tool (A)

Encourage your kids to read a newspaper (L, U, M, S)

Take a tour of a city's architecture (M, S)

Visit a National, state, county, or city Park (A)

"Ex"perience

Audition and perform a role in a theatrical production for a school production, local civic theater, or Children's theater (L, U, M, S)

Participate in a youth group's mission trip (M, S)

Work as a student reporter for a local newspaper or the student paper (M, S)

Shadow a reporter for a full or partial day (M, S)

Participate in an "Adopt-A-Mile" program to pick up trash (U, M, S)

Work with your child in developing a budget with their allowance (U, M, S)

Use and own a ATM Card (Automatic Teller Machine) (U, M, S)

Conduct an "Information Interview" with someone at their workplace (M, S)

Plant dune grass as part of an environmental project (U, M, S)

Take a tour of a factory (e.g., Coca-Cola, Hershey's, Kellogg's) or one in your local area (U, M)

Visit a TV or radio studio (U, M, S)

View educational TV programs, e.g., National Geographic's *Discovery* (U, M, S)

Attend "Open Houses" sponsored by local businesses (M, S)

Participate in planning or participating in a local parade (M, S)

Serve as a volunteer at the local hospital (S)

Become a school crossing guard (U)

Open up and monitor a checking or savings account (L, U, M, S)

Design, build, and race a soapbox derby and sew your clothes and fashions (M, S)

<u>"Ex"posure</u>

Visit your state's capitol building (M, S)

Travel, travel, travel (domestic or foreign) (A)

Attend or participate in a historical re-enactment (L, U, M)

Visit a fish hatchery (L, U, M, S)

Participate in constructing a "Habitat for Humanity" House (M, S)

Participate in an "Earth Day" project, e.g., cleaning up a littered river bank (M,S)

Visit a zoo (A)

Collect things, ranging from coins to car parts, from baseball cards to butterflies (L, U, M, S)

Visit a hospital (U, M, S)

Plant and tend a garden (M, S)

Create greeting cards (L, U, M, S)

<u>"Ex"perience</u>

Imagine and create your own jewelry (M, S)

Design and create your own clothes and fashions (M, S)

Produce a video as entertainment or a documentary (M, S)

Conduct an "oral history" on someone or something by recording on audio tape (M, S)

Volunteer in an archeological dig on a local excavation (S)

Write or edit a Neighborhood Newsletter (M, S)

Troubleshoot and repair a problem with an appliance, an electronic item, a bike, or a car (M, S)

Participate and attend a school's "Market Day" where students promote and sell products they made or manufactured as part of a school project (L, U, M)

Regularly check out the "Community Calendar" in your newspaper or local cable TV access channel and participate in selected events and activities (A)

Create your own computer program (U, M, S)

Visit an aircraft controller in their tower (M, S)

Spend a day(s) on a working farm (U, M)

Collect autographs/signatures of famous people by sending them individualized letters. Learn about each person prior to sending them your letter. (U, M, S)

Serve on a high school's "Teen Court" where student violations, ranging from parking offenses to carrying firearms on school grounds are dealt with. Students serve in real-life roles as a jurist, prosecuting or defense attorney, judge, or bailiff. Decisions are binding and cannot be appealed. (S)

"Ex"posure	"Ex"perience
Attend a funeral of a family member of a friend of the family (U, M, S)	
Attend a service in a church or synagogue (A)	Work as an interpreter for a social service agency. (S)
Attend a live, symphony concert (U, M, S)	
Volunteer as a Junior Docent at an area museum. (S)	
Observe a repair person, a carpenter, or a plumber who comes to your home to do a project (U, M, S)	Serve as a campaign volunteer for a political candidate. (S)
Be responsible for a family pet (L, U, M, S)	
Visit the Humane Society (A)	Run for office. Develop a campaign, seek volunteers, give speeches, etc. for any office in a club, student council, class office, or actual civic office (check out age requirements for this).(U, M, S)
Attend an Air Show (A)	
Tour a submarine, aircraft carrier, or Navy vessel (L, U, M, S)	After your child read a book (a novel or non-fiction) that made an impact on him/her, visit some of the sites referenced in the book and talk to people who now live in those places and get their perspective on the people, places, and events that happened there. (U, M, S)
Visit a Space Museum (L, U, M)	
Visit an airport (P, L, U)	
Visit your State Representative, Congressman's or Senator's office (U, M, S)	

Read the daily newspaper and watch the News (L, U, M, S)

Attend a City Council meeting (M, S)

Attend a School Board meeting (M, S)

Visit a fire station (P, L, U)

"Ex"posure

Write a government official, expressing an opinion (L, U, M, S)

Set up a bird feeder and/or a bird house, or some type of feeding stations for other animals (L, U, M)

Visit a nuclear reactor or a power plant (U, M, S)

Visit a Native American burial site or historic pictographs (U, M, S)

Visit and shop at an antique shop (U, M, S)

Design and make something out of Play-Doh (P, L)

Create and present a puppet show (L, U, M, S)

Visit and attend your State Fair or a County Fair (A)

Build and shoot off a model rocket (U, M)

Browse your local library (A)

Identify and conduct career information interviews with persons who are minorities (M, S)

Identify and conduct career information interviews with persons in non-traditional roles (M, S)

Participate in a school's "Wonderful Wednesdays" or "Fantastic February" program that sets aside some time (half-hour at noon or after school) to develop a particular skill (ethnic cooking, magic, cartooning, quilting, karate, etc.) (L, U, M)

"Ex"posure

Learn about different careers as it pertains to current topics being taught in schools. Encourage your teachers to host, in class, parents whose career reflects the material being taught, e.g., an environmental engineer speaks about ecology. (L, U, M, S)

Post a world map or purchase a globe and identify places as they're mentioned in the news. (L, U, M)

Attend Open Houses of new plants or additions to facilities (U, M, S)

Attend a Book Fair (L, U, M)

Check out garage sales (L, U, M)

Visit specialty shops, e.g., nature/ecology, pets, computers, plants, ethnic items, hiking/camping, etc., (L, U, M, S)

Develop a card catalog system either manually or on a PC that catalogs all their books or those of your family (M, S)
Go camping (L, U, M, S)

Attend and/or participate in a historical re-enactment, e.g., a Renaissance Faire, Civil War or Revolutionary War battle, etc. (U, M, S)

Participate in school field trips, either the 1 day or extended (3-14 days) variety (L, U, M, S)

Regularly review the "Computer" section in your newspaper that highlights new websites. (definitely worth checking out!)

"Ex"posure

Imagine with your child by painting "talking" pictures with them. Play with them by posing a lot of "imagine how" questions, such as "Imagine how it would be to be:
1) a TV reporter
2) a minister
3) an astronaut
4) an archeologist
5) a geologist
6) a web page designer
(P, L, U)

Serve as student representative on a Community Foundation or United Way (organization that dispenses funds for local projects or social service agencies) (S)

Participate in a Summer Reading program at the local library (P, L, U)

Read award-winning books, such as ones that receive the *Caldecott Medal for Illustration* and the *Newberry Medal for Writing* (P, L, U)

Visit different types of post-secondary institutions within a 100 mile radius of home. Check out the differences between small, medium, and large institutions; public and private; classical liberal arts and more vocationally-oriented. Nearly each institution has a special institute, museum, collection, laboratory, or arts facility that is renowned and open to the public. (M, S)

Develop a family tree and note the vocation of each family member. Check for patterns of careers, if any, from generation to generation. (U, M, S)

Appendix E

Information Interview Questions

Career______________________________

Name of person being interviewed______________________________

Date________________________________

1. Please tell me about your job. What do you like about what you do and what don't you like?

2. Who or what caused you to go into this type of work?

3. What type of training or education is necessary?

4. How, if at all, is technology used in your job?

5. How bright a future is there in this type of work?

6. What are the typical hours of your job?

7. How much flexibility do you have?

8. What does it take to be really successful in this type of work?

9. What gives you satisfaction in your job?

10. What are some related careers to what you do?

11. If you could do it all over again, would you select your career? Why or why not?

Appendix F

Multiple Intelligences/Career Links

When recognizing the inherent differences between various intelligences, it seems only appropriate that each intelligence is prone to attract or lend itself to distinctly different careers. The following lists indicate several careers that are approximate reflections of each of the nine intelligences as developed by Harvard University educator and researcher, Dr. Howard Gardner.

The careers are categorized by their dominant intelligence as identified through your completion of the eleven item *Multiple Intelligence Questionnaire* or the answers to questions 5-15 in Chapter 4. Each career that follows also recognizes two additional intelligences (in rank order) that complement the dominant intelligence. These additional intelligences are integral to the performance of the identified career. For instance, a "medical writer" reflects a *Verbal/Natural Science/Technology* multiple intelligence profile. In this career, "verbal" intelligence is the dominant intelligence followed by a "natural science" intelligence. A "technology" intelligence rounds out the profile.

The careers identified in these lists are courtesy of *Cool Careers for Dummies* (2nd Edition; published by Hungry Minds, Inc., ISBN: 0-7645-5345-3) by Marty Nemko and Paul & Sarah Edwards. This particular book is referenced since it cites careers where a likely demand for people will be strong in the future. The authors provide excellent descriptions that aid in describing the responsibilities and special challenges of each career.

When checking out various career options, review the list of careers in that are consistent with your child's dominant intelligence area. Focus on those careers that reflect a ranked sequence of your child's dominant intelligences to gage which careers are the most approximate matches. These careers warrant further investigation or consideration through readings, job shadowing, or information interviews (see Appendix E for questions used in information interviewing).

Again, it is important to note that the links between the intelligences and various careers are only approximations and not verified by empirical studies or analyses.

A. Verbal/Linguistic Intelligence

Verbal/linguistic are, as the name suggests, adept at leveraging words effectively whether that is in public speaking, writing, or everyday conversation. They enjoy reading and developing their vocabulary. They are particularly effective in offering expressing descriptions, explanations, or their opinions. Using various literary techniques such as story telling, metaphors, alliteration, or even poetry add to their linguistic arsenal. In speaking situations, they are equally sensitive to their non-verbal behavior as the words they employ. Today, more than ever, virtually all career fields require strong communication skills.

Legend:
V = Verbal/Linguistic
T = Technological/Math
E = Visual
A = Auditory/Musical
K = Kinesthetic/Physical/Motor
I = Interpersonal
S = Intrapersonal
N = Natural/Scientific
P = Philosophical/Religious

Career	Profile
Trial Consultant	V/T/I
Writer	V/S/E
Web Writer	V/T/E
Medical Writer	V/N/T
Journalist	V/I/E
Librarian	V/I/T
Corporate Intelligence Specialist	V/T/E
Television/Radio/Sports Announcer	V/I/T

Attorney	V/I/T
Sports Agent	V/I/T
Paralegal Assistant	V/T/I
Public Relations/Communications Specialist	V/I/E
Sports Information Specialist	V/I/T
Archivist	V/T/N
Historic Preservationist	V/E/T

B. Technological/Math Intelligence

Technological/Math-oriented individuals have a knack for thinking and problem solving in a systematic and logical fashion. Complex or ambiguous situations pose little difficulty for them. They can rely on infer, analyze, and calculate effectively. They also rely on technology as a necessary tool in their problem solving. For these individuals, reasoning rules.

Legend:
V = Verbal/Linguistic
T = Technological/Math/Logical
E = Visual
A = Auditory/Musical
K = Kinesthetic/Physical/Motor
I = Interpersonal
S = Intrapersonal
N = Natural/Scientific
P = Philosophical/Religious

Career	Profile
Computer Programmer	T/E/V
Web Programmer	T/E/V
Games Programmer	T/E/V
Computer Security Programmer	T/E/V
Avionics Technician	T/E/V
Electrician	T/K/V
Surveyor	T/V/K
Pharmacist	T/I/V
Web Designer	T/V/I
Accountant	T/V/I
Bank Officer	T/V/I
Geographic Information System Specialist	T/N/E

Pilot	T/E/V
Network Technician	T/V/E
Global Positioning Technician	T/E/N
Dental Hygienist	T/N/I
Cardiovascular Technician	T/N/V
Accident Reconstructor	T/E/V
Engineer (Mechanical, Manufacturing, Civil)	T/N/E
Quality Assurance Technician	T/N/E
FBI Agent	T/N/I
Online Educator	T/I/V
E-Commerce Specialist	T/E/I
Financial Planner	T/I/V

C. Visual Intelligence

Visual individuals see things just like anyone else—only better. They use their visual acuity to transform things as mundane as graphs and diagrams or as creatively as designing a new skyscraper. They have an uncanny sensitivity to unusual images, designs, colors, and textures. They can apply spatial concepts effectively. On a simple scale, they can get from A to B without asking directions. Most importantly, visual persons not only see things for what they are but for what they can be. Maybe, that's why they are called "visionaries."

Legend:
V = Verbal/Linguistic
T = Technological/Math/Logical
E = Visual
A = Auditory/Musical
K = Kinesthetic/Physical/Motor
I = Interpersonal
S = Intrapersonal
N = Natural/Scientific
P = Philosophical/Religious

Career	**Profile**
Image Consultant	E/I/V
Appraiser	E/T/V
Web Content Finder	E/T/V
Graphic Artist	E/T/I
Textile Designer	E/T/I
Technical Illustrator	E/V/T
Computer Aided Drafter	E/T/V
Chef	E/I/T
Optometrist	E/T/I

Dietician	E/T/I
Interior Designer	E/I/T
Cosmetologist	E/I/T
Fashion Designer	E/K/I
Photographer	E/I/T
Industrial Designer	E/T/I
Architect	E/T/I
Curator	E/V/T
Advertising Specialist	E/I/V
Product Marketing Specialist	E/T/V

D. Auditory/Musical Intelligence

No one would think that Mick Jagger and Amadeus Mozart have much in common, but they do. They both share a dominance in their auditory/musical intelligence. Such persons with this intelligence can easily attend to changes in volume, pitch, or rhythm. Such people can readily learn music or a second language. It's a talent shared by composers, musicians, and speech pathologists.

Legend:
V = Verbal/Linguistic
T = Technological/Math/Logical
E = Visual
A = Auditory/Musical
K = Kinesthetic/Physical/Motor
I = Interpersonal
S = Intrapersonal
N = Natural/Scientific
P = Philosophical/Religious

Career	Profile
Music Synthesizer	A/T/V
Musician	A/S/V
Composer	A/S/V
Foreign Language Translator	A/T/V
Acoustician	A/T/V
Audiologist	A/T/I
Speech Therapist	A/I/V

E. Kinesthetic/Motor Intelligence

Physical agility and strength are part and parcel for persons using this intelligence. Such people can use their intelligence in expressive, creative, and productive ways. Staying physically fit is an ongoing objective for persons leveraging this intelligence in their career. They are definitely "hands-on" kind of people.

Legend:
V = Verbal/Linguistic
T = Technological/Math/Logical
E = Visual
A = Auditory/Musical
K = Kinesthetic/Physical/Motor
I = Interpersonal
S = Intrapersonal
N = Natural/Scientific
P = Philosophical/Religious

Career	Profile
Tool & Die Maker	K/T/E
Computer Repair Technician	K/T/I
Millwright	K/T/E
Automobile Repair Technician	K/T/E
Athletic Trainer	K/N/T
Wellness Coordinator	K/V/E
Personal Trainer	K/N/I
Chiropractor	K/I/T
Tree Trimmer	K/N/T
Carpenter	K/E/T
Dancer	K/A/E
Plumber	K/T/I

F. Interpersonal Intelligence

"I like to work with people" would be an often-quoted comment from persons in the Interpersonal Intelligence group. These "people people" seem to have a knack for effectively dealing with others. They often demonstrate a lot of care and consideration for others. They are keen listeners and engaging conversationalists. Friendliness, empathy, and harmony are their traits. They also have a knack for discerning a person's motives. Having a high EQ (emotional quotient) is more important than one's IQ (intelligence quotient) for these good people.

Legend:
V = Verbal/Linguistic
T = Technological/Math/Logical
E = Visual
A = Auditory/Musical
K = Kinesthetic/Physical/Motor
I = Interpersonal
S = Intrapersonal
N = Natural/Scientific
P = Philosophical/Religious

Career	Profile
Mediator	I/V/M
Geriatric Caregiver	I/V/P
Psychotherapist	I/V/N
Sports Psychologist	I/V/K
Social Worker	I/V/S
Employment Interviewer	I/V/A
Events Planner	I/E/V
Exporter	I/V/A
City Manager	I/V/T

Human Resources Manager	I/V/T
School Administrator	I/V/S
Teacher	I/V/S
Corporate Trainer	I/V/T
Mediator	I/V/T
Politician	I/V/S
Occupational Therapist	I/T/V
Physician's Assistant	I/N/T
Physician	I/N/T
Dentist	I/N/T
Nurse/Nurse Practitioner	I/N/T
Paramedic	I/N/T
Physical Therapist	I/N/T
Prison Support Worker	I/V/K
Day Care Provider	I/V/A

G. Intrapersonal Intelligence

Rodin's *Thinker* is the poster-child for those with a dominance in intrapersonal intelligence. Why? It's because they ask a lot of "why" questions. Their pondering is mostly introspective. They contemplate their decisions, review their behaviors and innermost thoughts, and make careful plans and goals. Accompanying their self-analysis and personal reflection is usually a high degree of initiative. Their mantra is that of Aristotle: know thyself.

Legend:
V = Verbal/Linguistic
T = Technological/Math/Logical
E = Visual
A = Auditory/Musical
K = Kinesthetic/Physical/Motor
I = Interpersonal
S = Intrapersonal
N = Natural/Scientific
P = Philosophical/Religious

Career	Profile
Sales	S/I/V
Fundraiser	S/I/V
Actor	S/V/K

H. Naturalist/Scientific

Whether it's flora or fauna, fish or foul, the Naturalist has a love for yes, nature. A scientific curiosity allows the Naturalist to study the intricacies of the natural world, ranging from studying tissues to examining geologic faults. Applying their scientific studies for productive, profitable, or societal benefits helps motivate the Naturalist. They are advocates of scientific research, conservation, and promoting good health and environmental practices.

Legend:

V = Verbal/Linguistic
T = Technological/Math/Logical
E = Visual
A = Auditory/Musical
K = Kinesthetic/Physical/Motor
I = Interpersonal
S = Intrapersonal
N = Natural/Scientific
P = Philosophical/Religious

Career	**Profile**
Geneticist	N/T/E
Biologist	N/T/E
Toxicologist	N/T/E
Geologist	N/T/E
Adventure Travel Organizer	N/I/V
Arborist	N/T/K
Oceanographer	N/T/K
Landscape Architect	N/E/I
Park Ranger	N/I/K
Veterinarian	N/I/K
Chemist	N/T/E

Zoologist	N/T/E
Medical Researcher	N/T/E

I. Philosophical/Religious Intelligence

Considering the "larger" issues of life is something that motivates those with a preference for philosophical/religious intelligence. They provide a perspective that transcends most things. They embrace the questions that most of us mere mortals rarely ponder. For the theologian, their questioning provides an appreciation for God and hopefully some insights about the Almighty. For the philosopher, they offer an opinion that goes beyond the everyday and provides some meaning on the "why" of life. For the ethicist, they strive for a more just society both locally and globally.

Legend:
V = Verbal/Linguistic
T = Technological/Math/Logical
E = Visual
A = Auditory/Musical
K = Kinesthetic/Physical/Motor
I = Interpersonal
S = Intrapersonal
N = Natural/Scientific
P = Philosophical/Religious

Career	Profile
Ethicist	P/V/S
Theologian	P/V/S
Non-profit administrator	P/I/V
Clergy	P/V/S
Foreign Service Officer	P/V/I
Pollster	P/M/V

Bibliography

Armstrong, Thomas, *In Their Own Way,*

Barkley, Nella, *How to Help Your Child Land the Right Job,* New York: Workman Publishing, 1993

Byham, William, *Zapp!,* New York: Faucett Columbine, 1992

Covey, Stephen, *The 7 Habits of Highly Effective People,* New York: Fireside, 1993

Curran, Dolores, *Traits of a Healthy Family,* Minneapolis: Winston Press, 1983

Kerr, Barbara, *Career Planning for Gifted and Talented Youth,* ERIC Digest #E492, 1990

O'Connor, Elizabeth, *Eighth Day of Creation,* Washington, D.C.: The Servant Leadership School, 1971

Otto, Luther B., *Helping Your Child Choose a Career,* Indianapolis: JIST Works, Inc., 1996

Martin, Joyce, *Live and Work by Your Intelligences,* Training & Development, October, 1999

Michigan Department of Education (Center for Quality Special Education), *Special Education Program/Outcomes Guide: Emotional Impairment*, 1990

Michigan Department of Education (Center for Quality Special Education), *Unique Educational Needs of Learners with Specific Learning Disabilities,* 1992

Patterson, Ben, *Serving God,* Downers Grove, Illinois: InterVarsity Press, 1987

Schein, Edgar, *Career Anchors: Discovering your Real Values,* San Francisco: Jossey-Bass, 1993

Shearer, Branton, Multiple Intelligence Newsletters, Kent State University, Kent, Ohio; to receive the newsletters, contact (join-MI-News@ds.xc.org)

Tobias, Cynthia, *The Way They Learn,* Colorado Springs, Colorado: Focus on the Family, 1994

About the Author

Mark de Roo's professional background includes more than 20 years in human resources positions in manufacturing, education, and service industries, including positions with Herman Miller, Inc., Trans-Matic Manufacturing Co., and Manpower, Inc. He is President of Keystone Coaching & Consulting, LLC, a corporate coaching and human resources consulting service. He has coached over 800 individuals and numerous business, government, and non-profit organizations.

He holds a Master's degree from Western Michigan University and a Bachelor's degree from Hope College. He is a graduate of Corporate Coach University and has earned a Senior Professional in Human Resources (SPHR) designation.

He is married (Roxanne) and is father to Ingrid, Taylor, and Hillary. He is active in a variety of community and church activities. A favorite passion of his is mountain climbing. He has summitted the highest point in 47 of the 50 states in the United States.

0-595-26168-X

Made in the USA
Lexington, KY
07 January 2016